BLACK RIDERS

the Spirit is a bone.—HEGEL

Jerome McGann

BLACK RIDERS

The Visible Language of Modernism

PRINCETON UNIVERSITY PRESS · PRINCETON, NEW JERSEY

Library of Congress Cataloging-in-Publication Data

McGann, Jerome J.
Black riders : the visible language of modernism / Jerome McGann.
    p.   cm.
Includes index.
ISBN 0-691-06985-9 (CL : acid-free paper)
ISBN 0-691-01544-9 (PB : acid-free paper)
1. English poetry—20th century—History and criticism.
2. Modernism (Literature)   3. American Poetry—20th century—
History and criticism.   4. Morris, William, 1834–1896—Influence.
5. Visual poetry—History and criticism.   6. Book design—History.
7. Art and literature.   8. Printing—History.   I. Title.
PR478.M6M38   1993
821'.91091—dc20   92–29109 CIP

This book has been composed in Adobe Caslon

images consisting not only in words but also in objects and actions.

—SIMONE WEIL, "Reflections on Quantum Theory"

Minnie began to settle down. For a while all was quiet with Mickey there beside her. Then, turning to him with the beginning of a smile on her downy face: "Mickey," she said, "Did you hear that sound? I think we have mice in the house."

—*Mickey Mouse Comics*

Contents

List of Illustrations

Preface

THIS BOOK centers in an argument about the historical context of modernist writing. The argument holds that twentieth-century poetry in English is a direct function and expression of the Renaissance of Printing that began in the late nineteenth century. While various scholars of modernism have carried out specialized investigations of the bibliographical features of modernist writing, no one has heretofore attempted to explain those features in such particular historical terms.

In pursuing this argument I have had to explicate the cultural significance of "literalism"—called "the language of Adam" by earlier writers—as a recurrent preoccupation of recent imaginative work. Though Blake was modernism's first great "literalist of imagination," as Yeats acutely saw, my focus here begins with William Morris and the literalist traditions directly inaugurated by his work.

❀ Hold on a minute. What do you mean that you "have had to" do this? It seems to me no matter of necessity at all, but just something driven by your special interests. One could have made the historical argument without so much as touching on those other, more difficult and problematic, issues. The history and prehistory of modernism don't require a philosophical inquiry into poetic literalism and "the language of Adam."

No doubt—but then so much would have been lost to view. For this other part of the argument deepens the cultural implications involved, and demonstrates the significance of the historical presentation and materials. At the same time, it begins to expose the historical argument to critical attack. The attack cannot be avoided. The strength of the expository argument demands that we be clear about the limits of exposition as a form of argument.

We often think that the further an argument is developed (the more strongly elaborated and the more thoroughly exemplified) the more compelling it becomes. And while this result no doubt follows in one perspective, in another it does not follow at all. For when an argument seeks full self-development it begins to approach the horizon of its own truths, and hence begins to expose itself to disconfirmation and critique.

One expects to be challenged, argued with—perhaps even interrupted. To say anything at all is already to sketch the limits for what you have to say—as you in effect have just said. All texts run as difference engines. So one finds disconfirmation entering this book "literally," as a series of brief dialogical interventions that climax in the final reflexive turn: the dialogue that closes the body of this book. As this work unfolds, therefore, it weaves together two forms of critical thought, the one expository, the other dialectical.

The introduction and part I are largely devoted to a historical presentation of a poetic style of imaginative literalism (to adapt the phrase Marianne Moore famously adapted out of Yeats and Blake). The cases advanced are in every sense exemplary rather than comprehensive, for others could have been easily used. Some choices were dictated by historical necessity—like Morris and Yeats and Pound—but others came in for perhaps more personal or even political reasons. Important figures like Moore, Auden, Williams, and Oppen are relevant and might have been enlisted to support my argument, but they are barely if at all mentioned. Laura Riding, on the other hand, figures prominently in this book. She fits the historical presentation of part I no better (and no worse) than those other writers, but I wanted to bring her work forward because she has been so badly misunderstood and neglected. More importantly, her early appearance in this book's historical argument makes a useful link with the philosophical inquiry pursued in part II, where Riding is a crucial and probably unevadable presence.

In any case, the book moves from a largely "historical" demonstration to a largely "philosophical" inquiry. The philosophical import of the material presented in part I is developed and pursued in part II, where I investigate the relation of imaginative writing, knowledge, and truth. The issues here are of course highly problematic and open to dispute.

❋ To say the least.

Indeed. But this book wants to preserve a sharp awareness of the disputed issues. The pair of chapters in part II are cast into forms that display the volatile nature of the situation: chapter 3 is an aggressive polemic; chapter 4 is an uncertain and veering dialogue.

In all this I have been trying to study and determine what place poetry occupies in a world that is already hailing farewell to the book as we know it. Related to this problem is the function served today by philology and literary criticism. Let it be said here that I do not have solutions to these problems, or answers to the questions the problems raise.

❋ You have no views on these matters—ideas, perhaps even commitments? I don't believe it.

Clearly I do. Taking William Morris as a point of departure for a study of modernism involves more than a simple historical statement about twentieth-century poetry and its relation to the history of printing. Much could and should be said about Morris and his work in a general way. Our interest in theory of art has been dominated for so long by the conceptual forms of Enlightenment and romantic thought that we have forgotten the revolutionary character of his basic insight: that if we wish to understand art and poetry we have to approach them as crafts, as practical forms of making.

"You can't have art without resistance in the materials." This was Morris's artisanal insight, and it carries profound implications. We can trace these implications historically—for example, in the development of twentieth-century poetic practices. But we can also speculate on the cultural and philosophical implications of such an idea, were it to be taken as seriously as Morris (like Blake before him) took it. The second part of this book pursues speculations along these lines.

But while I do not doubt this work's (historical) knowledge or even the possibility of its (critical) truth, its own historical location must cast into darkness the traditional assumption made by cultural actions of this kind. For whereas the relation of poetry and culture was once taken for granted, that relation no longer seems certain, and it has grown more uncertain for the past two hundred years.

How difficult it has become to think clearly about art's place in the modern world! Surely no one has thought more clearly on these matters than Emanuel Levinas, yet even he continually lapses from his visionary humaneness into abstract and symbolic habits of thought. In his celebrated essay of 1948, for example, "Reality and its Shadow," he says that "the phenomenology of images [i.e., the language of art] insists on their transparency" (134).[1] To the contrary, the phenomenology of images insists on their obduracy—on an immediate and face value that forbids us to look through them toward something beyond, whether it be conceptual or referential. And who more than Levinas ought to have understood that? Morris, I think, never lost sight of this great truth once it dawned upon his consciousness. In their resort to "the phenomenology of images," art and poetry take their stand outside a patriarchal order of symbolic value and an economic order of exchange value.[2]

No one will find it an easy matter to escape those profane orders, least of all a book of this kind. What general cultural importance can be given to a study of the bibliographical features of modernist poetry? On the face of it, nothing could seem more pedantic. Great works of science and technology throw such investigations, as we say these days, entirely "into the margin." As they should.

And yet . . . and yet the very power of those other pursuits, with their clear importance for our daily lives, suggests why we might "sing amidst our uncertainty," as the poets still say. There are perhaps measures of truth to be discovered in conditions of alienation, measures that may answer to (and for) the confident lies that reach us every day from quotidian centers of power. Perhaps we need not *escape* into poetry and the study of poetry. Perhaps we may go there, briefly or otherwise, to recover models (touchstones even?) of knowing and truth-telling elsewhere lost—given the kind of world we inhabit, the kind of representatives we choose and presidents we have recently honored and elected.

Acknowledgments

FIRST, TO MY STUDENTS, thanks for the conversations; then to so many others who helped me through various parts of this book, and especially Gerald Bruns, Cheryl Guiliano, Marjorie Perloff, Jeffrey Skoblow, Pat Spacks, Chip Tucker.

Bob Von Hallberg gave the book a long and searching critique for which I am very grateful, as I am for the equally helpful criticisms from those anonymous angels, the press readers.

Thanks as well to the editors of *Critical Inquiry*, the *Huntington Library Quarterly*, and *Postmodern Culture* for publishing parts of this book. I am also grateful to the Houghton Library for allowing me to reproduce here facsimiles of their Emily Dickinson manuscripts.

I wish to thank Susan Bee, Charles Bernstein, Alan Davies, Lyn Hejinian, and Susan Howe for permission to quote from their work; and Jonathan Williams for permission to quote from his Jargon/Corinth Books edition of Robert Carlton Brown's *1450–1950*. Also quoted with permission are the following:

"The Point"; "Untitled"; and "If wants to be the same" © 1988 by David Bromige. Reprinted from *Desire* with the permission of Black Sparrow Press.

Robert Frost, "The Gift Outright," quoted with permission of Henry Holt Company.

Laura Riding Jackson excerpts from *The Telling* quoted with permission of Harper Collins Publishers. Thanks also to Persea Books Inc., for passages from Laura (Riding) Jackson's poems "When Love Becomes Words," "Poet: A Lying Word," and "The Life of the Dead." In conformity with the late author's wish, her Board of Literary Management asks us to record that, in 1941, Laura (Riding) Jackson renounced, on grounds of linguistic principle, the writing of poetry: she had come to hold that "poetry obstructs general attainment to something better in our linguistic way-of-life than we have."

Gertrude Stein, from *Stanzas in Meditation*, quoted with permission of Yale University Press.

Wallace Stevens, "The Reader," quoted with permission from Alfred A. Knopf, Inc.

William Butler Yeats, from *The Oxford Book of Modern Verse, 1892–1935*, quoted with permission from Oxford University Press.

Emily Dickinson manuscript texts: reprinted by permission of the publishers from *The Manuscript Books of Emily Dickinson*, Vols. I and II, edited by R. W. Franklin, Cambridge, Mass.: The Belknap Press of Harvard University Press. Copyright © 1951, 1955, 1978, 1979, 1980 by the President and Fellows of Harvard College. © 1914, 1924, 1929, 1932, 1935, 1942 by Martha Dickinson Bianchi.

Emily Dickinson typescript texts: reprinted by permission of the publishers and the Trustees of Amherst College from *The Poems of Emily Dickinson*, Thomas H. Johnson, ed., Cambridge, Mass.: The Belknap Press of Harvard University Press. Copyright © 1951, 1955, 1979, 1983 by the President and Fellows of Harvard College.

The monochrome copies of pages from William Morris's *A Book of Verse* are reproduced by courtesy of the Board of Trustees of the Victoria and Albert Museum.

Finally there are those who have been keeping the divine vision in this time of trouble. They are many, and I name but a few who have been especially important for me in this work: Charles Bernstein, David Bromige, Virgil Burnett, Alan Davies, Susan Howe, Janet Kauffman, Steve McCaffery.

BLACK RIDERS

Introduction

Modernism and the Renaissance of Printing, with Particular Reference to the Writing of Yeats, Stein, and Dickinson

I go to see my noble and learned brother pretty well every day, when he sits in the Inn. He don't notice me, but I notice him. There's no great odds betwixt us. We both grub on in a muddle.

—CHARLES DICKENS, *Bleak House*

No PASSAGE in Yeats's work is more famous than the final stanza of "The Circus Animals' Desertion." The lines are with good reason read as a kind of aesthetic testament—Yeats's late reflections on the nature of poetry, particularly his own poetry.

> These masterful images because complete
> Grew in pure mind but out of what began?[1]

He answers that question with a series of memorable images, culminating in the final, celebrated "foul rag and bone shop of the heart."

Of course no one mistakes the discursive meaning of the passage. Auden later appropriated Yeats's text in order to illustrate "what every artist knows[,] that the sources of his art are 'the foul rag-and-bone shop of the heart,' its lusts, its hatreds, its envies."[2] That is the standard line of ethically thematized interpretation, most recently repeated in Daniel Albright's commentary on Yeats's figure of the rag and bone shop: "Yeats's most abject term for the *Anima Mundi*, the imagination's storehouse of images, now relocated in a private slum."[3]

Albright is correct to speak of a "slum" in relation to the line, because that image turns back to the earlier images in the stanza and emphasizes the "completeness" of this passage's own "masterful image." "The Circus Animals' Desertion" closes, that is to say, in a sharply located scene: not merely in "a private slum," but in a certain kind of commercial shop on a certain kind of street. When Dickens took us to that place, in *Bleak House*, the "till" was kept not by a "raving slut" but by the grotesque, if equally unforgettable, Mr. Krook.

In all the commentary no one seems to have asked why Yeats chose to associate the "heart" of poetry with that *particular* image of commercial activity, the rag and bone shop. After all, other figures of foulness and the *Anima Mundi* were available to Yeats. What led him to draw this figure into his poem? Or perhaps I should not frame the problem in exactly that fashion, for it assumes too close a relation between poetic intention and poetic result. So: whatever was in Yeats's mind when he was writing this poem,[4] what poetic consequence follows from choosing the rag and bone shop image?

All the commentary on the passage assumes the same answers to these questions. Like Krook's rag and bottle shop, Yeats's rag and bone shop is seen as an image of human life in its least exalted mood. Henry Mayhew has an extensive discussion "of the Street-Buyers of Rags, Broken Metal, Bottles, Glass, and Bones" in his *London Labour and the London Poor*.[5] His description of the interior of the rag and bone shop anticipates Yeats's epithet "foul."

> The stench in these shops is positively sickening. Here in a small apartment may be a pile of rags, a sack-full of bones, the many varieties of grease and "kitchen-stuff," corrupting an atmosphere which, even without such accompaniments, would be too close. . . . The inmates seem unconscious of this foulness. (II. 108)

This is the rag and bone shop of Yeats's commentators, and it clearly corresponds to important features in the poem. But it is not all that might or should be understood about the slum business that Yeats's text has summoned and recalled.

Once again Mayhew is helpful for giving a closer view of the rag and bone shop's commercial function. He supplies a great deal of information about the location and contents of such establishments, and he even sketches the structure of some of their commercial relations. We learn, for example, that these shops were serviced by itinerant refuse pickers, some of whom might be the proprietors of the shops themselves. More significantly, we also learn that the most valuable and important material in the shops were the rags, for which the shop owner was prepared to pay significant prices—especially if the rags were of high quality (e.g., linen rags).

Rags were the most important material bought and sold in the rag and bone shop because they were, particularly in the nineteenth century, in very high demand. Bones were used for fertilizer; metal, bottles, and glass were recycled; and the rags were sold either to stationers or to the great paper merchants, who would reprocess them to make paper. In this context Yeats's "foul rag and bone shop" accumulates to itself a whole set of particular associations and relations that are highly significant for a text that has made this slum shop a foundational figure in a poetical manifesto.

When Yeats imagines the Jacob-ladder of poetry starting in a working class establishment that supplies material for papermaking, his mind is working as a nineteenth-century romantic mind. The immediate historical allusion is not to papermaking in general, but to printers and publishers who used a certain kind of paper (rag paper) and made a certain kind of book (fine-press printing). By the end of the nineteenth century, rag paper was almost never used by the regular printing trade. It was too expensive. Whereas before the Victorian period English printers used pure rag or rag-based paper,[6] by the end of the century rag paper was used only for ornamental and deluxe books.[7]

The handcrafted books produced at the Cuala Press, for example, were all printed on rag paper,[8] and so were the books turned out by Kelmscott and the other fine-printing houses which sprang up at the end of the nineteenth century.[9] These presses, it is important to remember, were specifically founded as part of an effort to return to an earlier, craft-based method of book production—an effort to step aside from the processes and products of the age of mechanical reproduction.

Even before the founding of the Cuala Press, Yeats had conceived his work in this bibliographical tradition. Two of his most admired precursors, William Blake and William Morris, occupied key positions in that romantic tradition of printing based in the (ultimately medieval) arts and crafts processes of the handmade book. The Dun Emer Press was established in 1902 by Elizabeth Yeats at the urging of Emery Walker—the man who had been the immediate inspiration behind the founding of Morris's epochal Kelmscott Press.

Walker sent Elizabeth Yeats to London to study typography and book design at the Women's Printing Society, and when she returned to Ireland she, along with her sister Lily, began to produce the famous series of Dun Emer and Cuala Press books, the first of which was her brother's *In the Seven Woods* (1904).[10] Walker was the press's typographical advisor and Yeats served as chief editor. The entire venture was consciously planned as an Irish continuation of the project first imagined and executed by Morris with his Kelmscott Press. As Robin Skelton remarks, the Yeats's press moved off from "Emery Walker's ideas on printing, and Morris's ideas on the place of the arts in society.[11]

The final line of "The Circus Animals' Desertion" thus intersects with an extremely important historical tradition, so far as poetry is concerned. Yeats takes his place in that tradition via his involvement with the fine-press work of the Dun Emer and Cuala Presses, which played a crucial role in the late nineteenth- and early twentieth-century's massive act of bibliographical resistance to the way poetry was being materially produced. It is a familiar (and a romantic) history of historical change and defiance of historical change; and one strand of that history involves the evolution of papermaking in the industrial age.

Odd as it might at first glance seem, the rag and bone shop represents the "heart" of that secondary history. Yeats's poem exploits the shop's romantic possibilities—as Dickens's novel, earlier, did not. The difference between the entirely unromantic presentation of the shop in *Bleak House*, and Yeats's ironical and nostalgic approach, must be traced to the historical catastrophe which overtook such shops between the mid-Victorian period and 1890. Mayhew tells us that these shops could be found in abundance throughout the poorer districts of the cities and towns of Great Britain: one or even two shops might operate on any given street. They were there because they were needed by the stationers and printers. Indeed, book, periodical, and newspaper production increased so dramatically in the early nineteenth century that the demand for rags became acute, and supplies were constantly falling short. As a consequence, entrepreneurs were vigorously seeking ways to reduce the need for rags in papermaking.

At mid-century, when Mayhew was publishing his classic studies of working-class life, the rag and bone shop was still much in evidence, even though important mechanical innovations in paper-making had already taken place in the first part of the century. But as yet no good substitute had been found for rags. This came after mid-century, especially in the 1860s and 1870s (in Great Britain), when paper made from processed wood pulp utterly transformed the printing industry.[12] Between that period and 1937, when Yeats wrote "The Circus Animals' Desertion," this commercial revolution had made the rag and bone shop scarce enough to become a romantic figure of a lost world.

The explosion of fine-press printing in the late nineteenth century came as a movement of resistance against this new current of commercial book production. Kelmscott, Doves, Eragny, Cuala: these were the kind of social and commercial organizations which remained in contact with the disappearing rag and bone shops. Their books needed the rag paper that had been traditionally supplied by the rags collected in those shops. In "The Circus Animals' Desertion," consequently, the rag and bone shop reappears as the sign of an original allegiance. Like Wordsworth's leech-gatherer, it is a nostalgic figure harking back to a particular form of social life that had come under threat of extinction from those powers that seemed so inimical to men like Blake, Ruskin, Morris—and Yeats.

It is, needless to say, a figure of particular importance to modernist poets. It calls our attention, once again, to the Pre-Raphaelite and Aesthetic roots of modernism, whose principal means of production in its formative years was commonly through small press and finely printed books. From Yeats and Pound to Stein and Williams and the writers of the Harlem Renaissance, fine-printing work, the small press, and the decorated book fashioned the bibliographical face of the modernist world. The foul rag and bone shop, paradoxically, is a peculiarly apt Yeatsian figure for the "heart" of that world.

Yeats's nostalgia in "The Circus Animals' Desertion" reflects—as the poem's two previous titles would have it—his "despair" "on the lack of a theme."[13] This felt conceptual poverty was more than overbalanced, as we have seen, by the work's abundant memorial materials; and the latter would be reinforced when the poem finally appeared in Yeats's *Last Poems and Two Plays*. Published in June, 1939 by Cuala Press, the book had been conceived by Yeats in

December, 1938, a month before his death.[14] The Cuala Press format is particularly important for this poem because the book supplies the text with a bibliographical environment that carries a general allusion to preindustrial social orders and artisanal bookwork.

In all works issued by Dun Emer/Cuala Press, Yeats's rag and bone shop is plainly visible at the material level of production. Established, as we have noted, under the direct influence of Kelmscott Press, the medievalism of the latter appears in Dun Emer/Cuala's slightly antiqued graphic style. The Dun Emer/Cuala colophons, printed in red, echo the manner of Kelmscott (the first of the colophons, for *In the Seven Woods*, was executed under the specific direction of Kelmscott Press's Sidney Cockerell).[15] As late arrivals to the Renaissance of Printing inaugurated in the nineteenth century, Dun Emer/Cuala Press books also exhibit their romanticism very directly. The small Pre-Raphaelite woodcuts that decorate the half titles, titles, and other pages indicate the conscious belatedness of these books, which are romantic at a second level—the way the poetic styles of Laetitia Elizabeth Landon or Winthrop Mackworth Praed or Thomas Lovell Beddoes were romantic at a second level in the 1820s (see fig. 1).

It is important to realize that these books might have looked very different, especially given Yeats's own history. They might, for example, have looked more like a Vale Press or a Bodley Head book. Yeats initially thought to work with Vale Press in the printing of his 1895 collected *Poems*,[16] for example, and he was himself a Bodley Head author, much involved with publishers like John Lane and Elkin Mathews and with the writers, artists, and printers who comprised the Aesthetic movement of the 1890s. Morris and Pre-Raphaelitism stand behind that movement, of course, just as they had been exerting a deep influence on its correspondent breeze, the Celtic Revival. Yet the dominant style of the 1890s derives not from Morris and Kelmscott, but from writers like Wilde, artists like Beardsley, and printers like Walter Blaikie. The defining cultural texts of the period are probably not an integral work of imagination like (say) *Tess of the d'Urbervilles* (1892) or *The importance of being earnest* (1895)—so typical of the period as these works are—but the famous Bodley Head periodical *The Yellow Book* and Vale Press's *The Dial*. As works of "visible language," both are utterly different from what Kelmscott produced or aspired to (see figs. 2 and 3).

LAST POEMS AND TWO PLAYS
BY WILLIAM BUTLER YEATS.

THE CUALA PRESS
DUBLIN IRELAND
MCMXXXIX

1. W. B. Yeats, *Last Poems and Two Plays*, title page, Cuala Press Edition (1939).

The Yellow Book

An Illustrated Quarterly

Volume I   April 1894

London : Elkin Mathews
& John Lane
Boston : Copeland &
Day

2. *The Yellow Book*, Vol. I, title page (1894).

THE BOOK

OF THE

RHYMERS' CLUB

LONDON
ELKIN MATHEWS
AT THE SIGN OF THE BODLEY HEAD
IN VIGO STREET
1892

3. *The Book of the Rhymers' Club*, title page (1892).

Readers who follow their texts primarily with an inner eye tend to see all "fine press" or "privately printed" books as more or less equivalent productions—varying perhaps only in their technical artistic achievements. To the extent that such bookmaking foregrounds the importance of writing's signifiers, the work exhibits uniformities and coherences. Different presses, however, generate distinctive sets of textual signifiers, and Yeats was well aware of the differences from the beginning of his career. Two of the most significant presses of the 1890s—Kelmscott and Bodley Head—carry unique and definite paratextual messages. Both share the view that meaning invests a work at the level of its physical appearance and linguistic signifiers, but each has in mind a different range of signifieds. Though both styles exhibit a kind of (as it were) poetic nominalism, the medievalism of Kelmscott does not correspond to the crisp aura of contemporaneity constructed by Bodley Head books (see figs. 4 and 5).

In this context we can more easily measure the significance of the bibliographical style of Dun Emer/Cuala Press books. The colophons are decisive.

> HERE END THE GREEN HELMET
> AND OTHER POEMS BY WILLIAM
> BUTLER YEATS. PRINTED AND
> PUBLISHED BY ELIZABETH COR-
> BET YEATS AT THE CUALA PRESS,
> CHURCHTOWN, DUNDRUM, IN
> THE COUNTY OF DUBLIN, IRE-
> LAND. FINISHED ON THE LAST
> DAY OF SEPTEMBER, IN THE
> YEAR NINETEEN HUNDRED AND
> TEN.

Squared off and printed in red, this colophon declares that the (Celtic) writing in the book is no mere conceptual undertaking. It has been made a deliberate and even a performative feature of a text whose every material part has been acquired, conceived, and executed in a "Celtic" world. As already noted, it is a colophon whose style was taken directly from the Kelmscott Press manner. The same style is evident in the first book issued by Dun Emer Press, *In the Seven Woods* (1903). The opening poem has its title printed in red and its text in black, a distinct recollection of Kelmscott work; and the material of the poetry is pure Celtic (see fig. 6 [monochrome]).

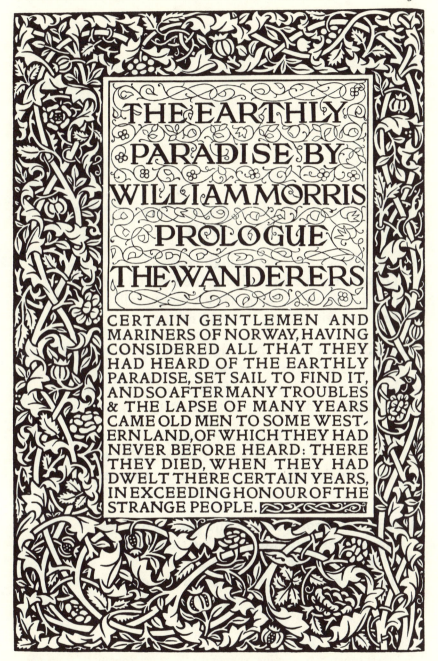

4. William Morris, *The Earthly Paradise*, "Prologue. The Wanderers," prose Argument (Kelmscott edition, 1896).

[10]

CARMELITE NUNS OF THE PERPETUAL ADORATION

Calm, sad, secure; behind high convent walls;
   These watch the sacred lamp, these watch and pray :
And it is one with them, when evening falls;
   And one with them, the cold return of day.

These heed not time : their nights and days they make
   Into a long, returning rosary;
Whereon their lives are threaded for Christ's sake :
   Meekness and vigilance and chastity.

A vowed patrol, in silent companies,
   Life long they keep before the living Christ :
In the dim church, their prayers and penances,
   Are fragrant incense to the Sacrificed.

Outside, the world is wild and passionate;
   Man's weary laughter, and his sick despair
Entreat at their impenetrable gate :
   They heed no voices in their dream of prayer.

5. Ernest Dowson, "Carmelite Nuns of the Perpetual Adoration," from *The Book of the Rhymers' Club* (1892).

IN THE SEVEN WOODS: BEING POEMS CHIEFLY OF THE IRISH HEROIC AGE.

IN THE SEVEN WOODS

I have heard the pigeons of the Seven Woods
Make their faint thunder, and the garden bees
Hum in the lime tree flowers; and put away
The unavailing outcries and the old bitterness
That empty the heart. I have forgot awhile
Tara uprooted, and new commonness
Upon the throne and crying about the streets
And hanging its paper flowers from post to post,
Because it is alone of all things happy.
I am contented for I know that Quiet
Wanders laughing and eating her wild heart
Among pigeons and bees, while that Great Archer,
Who but awaits His hour to shoot, still hangs
A cloudy quiver over Parc-na-Lee.

August, 1902.

THE OLD AGE OF QUEEN MAEVE

Maeve the great queen was pacing to and fro,
Between the walls covered with beaten bronze,
In her high house at Cruachan; the long hearth,
Flickering with ash and hazel, but half showed
Where the tired horse-boys lay upon the rushes,
Or on the benches underneath the walls,
In comfortable sleep; all living slept

b

6. W. B. Yeats, *In the Seven Woods*, opening text page, Dun Emer Press edition (1903).

If a Kelmscott approach dominated the graphic conception of Dun Emer/Cuala Press books—and it did—the Bodley Head style remains discernible in them. Both styles were obviously associated, in different historical ways, with the Celtic Revival; and while Yeats sought out Cockerell and Walker for advice about book design and production, the basic typographical style (as opposed to the general graphic design) of Dun Emer/Cuala books is closer to Bodley Head than it is to Kelmscott. That is to say, the books from the Yeats's press are not closely printed in faces that recall medieval manuscripts and tight fifteenth-century printing styles. The Dun Emer/Cuala typeface is a modern Caslon, and the lines of text are generously leaded to deliver—in contrast to Kelmscott books—an easily read page.

Unlike Morris before him, or Pound later, Yeats did not use his bibliographical models and forebears to fashion new artistic effects out of the material features of his Dun Emer/Cuala Press books. The latter are, in this respect, derivative works, as one sees from the relatively insignificant place they hold, as books, in either the history of printing or the history of literature (in contrast, for example, to the books of Blake, Dickens, Morris, Lear, Whitman, Pound or—as has yet to be properly recognized—Emily Dickinson). If Dun Emer/Cuala Press books were not technically innovative, however, they were well designed and quite successful. Cuala Press continued to publish for many years. This effectiveness arose out of the Yeats's clarity of purpose in founding the press. Commenting on the failure in 1907 of the Irish nationalist quarterly magazine *Shanachie*, Yeats criticized the work's lack of conceptual focus: "I don't believe it is possible to make a good magazine without making up your mind who it is for whom you are making it and keeping to that idea throughout" (*Letters*, 474). For Yeats, the same principle would have to cover a publishing imprint.

From the outset Dun Emer/Cuala kept its audience and purposes sharply in mind. These were quite different from the goals, for example, of Sir Charles Gavin Duffy's "New Irish Library," which Duffy launched in 1892 as a continuation of his earlier (and immensely successful) "Library of Ireland" books published in cheap formats in the 1840s as part of the Young Ireland movement. Duffy's ideas were too directly political and egalitarian for Yeats, whose different views were clearly set down in his 1895 anthology *A Book of Irish Verse*:

> This book differs also from some of its kind [i.e., the New Irish Library books], in being intended only a little for English readers, and not at all for Irish peasants, but almost wholly for the small beginning of that educated and national public, which is our greatest need and perhaps our vainest hope. (xxvii)

The Dun Emer/Cuala Press venture emerged from these ideas, as Yeats declared in various prefaces to the books printed at his sister's press.[17]

As it happened, the bifurcated allegiance coded bibliographically in the Dun Emer/Cuala Press book—to the medievalism of Kelmscott Press, on one hand, and to the contemporaneity of Bodley Head on the other—appears once again in Yeats's editorial and publishing goals. Working so closely in the 1890s with John Lane and Elkin Mathews, Yeats gained first-hand experience of how successful a small-press publishing venture could be if one carefully gauged and targeted the audience.[18] This is what Bodley Head did. An altogether less shrewd or commercially efficient operation, Kelmscott Press nonetheless seems to have convinced Yeats, among other things, that the kind of audience he wanted might be secured in Ireland. As a romantic socialist, Morris (famously) lamented that his work mainly catered to "the swinish luxury of the rich."[19] He pursued it nonetheless to the end, in the (sharp) teeth of the contradiction he clearly understood. As a romantic nationalist, Yeats saw no need for lament on this score. Lady Gregory was exactly the kind of reader and patron he wanted.

For most of his career Yeats evolved an interesting three-level procedure for transmitting his works. After first printing in a periodical or anthology, he would then gather some poems for publication in two distinct book formats: the private press Dun Emer/Cuala format, and the commercial Macmillan format. The Macmillan collections augmented or otherwise changed the poems first issued in the Dun Emer/Cuala Press books. From a purely rhetorical point of view, this method of production secured an extremely wide and various audience for his work. Having established his modernity in the 1890s, Yeats then settled into an effective publishing pattern. This began with the founding of Dun Emer Press in 1903. His transmission practices were designed to keep his poetry in continuous contact with bourgeois, (aristocratic) provincial, and avant-garde audiences, and he was careful to maintain and extend his European and American connections as well.

Yeats had, in this respect, clearly overgone the lead of William Morris, whose expensive Kelmscott books were typically issued in trade formats as well. Yeats's more elaborate method of dissemination shows how much he had learned from his association with Bodley Head. Lane and Mathews had developed procedures for defining specific audiences along other than simple economic lines. Morris's two-level method of publication was a pure economic convenience. Though by no means indifferent to economic concerns, Lane and Mathews were trying to imagine their audience(s) along cultural and ideological lines. Yeats's comment on the failure of *Shanachie* testifies to his understanding of these matters.

The peculiar style—and effectiveness—of Yeats's method of disseminating his work appears if we contrast it (for example) with the way an aesthetic writer like Dowson put his work into circulation, or with Gertrude Stein's early publication history (up to 1933), or even with Pound. As I shall later be discussing in detail the important case of Pound, let me comment briefly on the other two. Dowson, like Lionel Johnson and most of the 1890s aesthetes, reached print through the specialized organs of the "Yellow Nineties," and they did not make practical efforts to find an audience beyond that sphere. Yeats did. Furthermore, the writing scene in Great Britain had altered drastically with the turn of the century. Morris was dead, Bodley Head had suffered a divorce, and the trial of Oscar Wilde had seriously weakened the cultural influence of the Aesthetic movement and its artistic experiments. When Dun Emer began publishing in 1903, its cultural politics were provincial and conservative in ways that Kelmscott and Bodley Head had never been.

The situation in the United States ran a more or less parallel course. Close publishing connections were maintained between, for example, Bodley Head and the adventurous new American firm of Copeland and Day; Thomas Mosher kept alive the spirit of Morris and Pre-Raphaelitism, and the larger publishers also worked in concert with each other. When Pound arrived on the London scene in 1908, his American imagination was still fired with Pre-Raphaelitism and Aestheticism. Those inheritances supplied Pound and many other early modernists with the "determination to discover new modes of poetic expression."[20]

In 1910 a writer's allegiance to poetic experiment and innovation had to display some clear line of connection to the recent traditions that had inaugurated such work. Part of Pound's success in England must be traced to his Pre-Raphaelite commitments. Pound helped to bring forth a new avant-garde by marrying what we now call "modernism" to the writing of the late nineteenth century. Gertrude Stein, however—a far more innovative writer than Pound or perhaps anyone else writing in English during the first two decades of this century—remained for years a marginal and self-published author. Paradoxically, she never imagined that her work was meant for anything but a wide and even a popular audience.[21]

That paradox locates part of her problem. As an experimentalist she saw her work printed by avant-garde magazines and small presses. But for all the fame she achieved in Paris in the 1920s, her writing was difficult to locate or characterize (except through parody). As a consequence, even in the context of early modernism her work seemed (and still seems) sui generis, and its oddness is reflected in its printing history. Until her move into self-publication, her books do not have the kind of publication continuities we can trace so easily in Yeats or Pound or Eliot.

As a modernist writer, Stein occupied the margin of the margins. This position is clear from the outset. *Three Lives* (1909) went in search of a publisher for over a year before it was accepted by Grafton, a vanity press that only agreed to take the book if Stein paid for its costs. *Tender Buttons* (1914) was published in New York by Donald Evans's Claire Marie Press, which lasted a year. Evans's press distinctly cultivated an 1890s Aesthetic mode, as its titles—six seem to have been issued—indicate. They include Evans's own *Sonnets from the Patagonian: The Street of Little Hotels*, Allen Norton's *Saloon Sonnets: with Sunday Flutings*, and Mitchell S. Buck's *Syrinx: Pastels of Hellas*. Stein did not move in Evans's circle, however, nor does *Tender Buttons* display remarkable connections with the other works bearing the Claire Marie imprint. A Wildean character, Evans was the central figure of an upscale bohemian group that included not Stein but Wallace Stevens. Stevens's Parnassian manner recalls his early involvement with Evans and his friends, whose French connection was quite strong; and although Stein would become so famous in the expatriate American scene in Paris of the 1920s, she had little in common with the *symboliste* mode cultivated by Evans's circle.[22]

In the last phase of her career, when *The Autobiography of Alice B. Toklas* (1933) gave her access to the most reputable commercial publishers, her importance as a writer was once again evaded, this time by the academy. The period began with Stein issuing the Plain Editions of her works in 1931 in the fond hope and even expectation that the venture would prove a commercial success. She also knew that she had little choice, given her odd position in the "modernist" cultural scene. Although her work would be accepted by one or another of the avant-garde magazines of the 1920s, she had difficulty gaining any printed presence beyond them. Even when a key figure like Robert McAlmon was brought to sponsor one of her works, problems seemed inevitably to arise. McAlmon's Contact Edition of *The Making of Americans* (1925) proved a disaster in nearly every way. Neither Pound nor Eliot, for example, liked (or perhaps understood) her writing. In 1927 Eliot would denounce it as a threatening form of cultural barbarity.[23] Of course there were other more adventurous souls—Carl Van Vechten, Robert Carlton Brown—who did grasp what she was doing, as we shall see. Because they were (and would become, for the academy) marginal figures themselves, Stein remained culturally isolated. Not until she allowed herself to be transformed into a kind of circus animal, in the 1930s, would her writing find acceptance in regular publishing venues. Yet her popularity would at that point prove an obstacle in its own right. As the academy accepted the task of constructing the monument of modernism, Stein's writing was soon lost to sight. It seemed now to have fallen through a hole at the cultural center.

The publication history of Stein's work, so different from that of Yeats, is nonetheless equally and analogously instructive. The innovative conventions of printing and publishing established in the late nineteenth-century's Renaissance of Printing were taken up and extended by the modernists. Unlike the writing of Yeats and Pound, however, Stein's made its way through the modernist scene only with great difficulty. The Renaissance of Printing had encouraged writers to explore the expressive possibilities of language's necessary material conditions. These conditions were both broadly institutional (the publishing scene) and immediately physical (book design). The free forms of modernism—and Stein's are among the freest of those forms—depend upon the writerly exploitation of the spatial field of the printed page and codex form. More than this, the Renaissance of Printing also encouraged freedom and innovation in the publishing and distribution of texts—moves that, as we have seen, might ultimately be managed for the creation and consolidation of an audience of readers.

Stein's experimentalism was therefore licensed by the cultural scene in which she moved. That her work should have proved so problematic in that scene—which Yeats and Pound and Eliot negotiated with relative ease—signals the historical limits within which modernist experimentalism operated. Stein's *Stanzas in Meditation* (1933), perhaps the most neglected work of English-language modernism, would be inconceivable without the late-Victorian Renaissance of Printing, just as Pound's *Cantos* and Yeats's "The Circus Animals' Desertion" are inconceivable outside the same context.

🔳 "Stein's *Stanzas in Meditation* . . . inconceivable without the late-Victorian Renaissance of Printing?" What can you possibly mean? Stein's poem wasn't even printed in her lifetime.[24] Besides, it doesn't call for typographical manipulations or expressive page design. It's straightforward free verse in five sections. Nor is there anything particularly remarkable about its parts. They're divided into stanzas of varying lengths, and the sections have 15, 19, 21, 24, and 83 stanzas respectively. Period.

What else could one expect? None of Stein's works are especially interesting or important for their graphic elements or "visible language."

❊ Don't misread the aesthetic significance of the Renaissance of Printing. Brecht's epic theater and Stein's writing are both part of its legacy. Self-conscious text production like that of Kelmscott and Bodley Head put a frame around romantic writing (as Brecht threw a frame around realistic drama) and thereby brought important constructivist and reflexive elements to the scene of textuality. As a consequence, the (stylistic) conventions of romanticism were sharply modified. Writing lost both its fate and its faith in personal geography—that affective dialogue of spontaneous overflow, on one hand, with internal colloquy and recollection on the other. In a self-consciously constructed book, the romantic scene discloses itself as a rhetorical display: not the dialogue of the mind with itself, but the theatrical presentation of such a dialogue.

As you say, Stein did not utilize the physical presence of the book in any notable ways. But she developed linguistic (as opposed to bibliographical) procedures for bringing the reader's attention back to the text's literal surfaces and immediate moments. Her technical adventure was to find linguistic equivalents for the bibliographical innovations that were being developed and explored by others.

The very title of *Stanzas in Meditation* involves a play of syntax pointing to "Stanzas" as the true "subject" of the work. Stein's "Stanzas" are little rooms of words of a continuous conversation ("I could go on with this" [83]; "I will begin again yesterday" [127]).

> *Stanza XXIX*
> A stanza should be thought
> And if which can they do
> Very well for very well
> And very well for you.   (116)

This is not a "poetry of meditation" such as one follows in Herbert or Wordsworth. Stein's text is imagined as having a life of its own—indeed, as having many lives of its own (each life momently "named" with a number and located as a stanza in a continuous process of writing).

> *Stanza XVII*
> Not only this one now   (58)

Stein's texts prevent (spatial) distinctions between (manifest) surface and (concealed) significance, or (temporal) distinctions between past and present, memory and experience. The writing unfolds a continuous scene of multiplying transformations.

❧ But the little rooms are airless, unpeopled—like in Swinburne. Trace texts, nonreferential.

❀ One would do better to call them referentially "open." The pronouns dramatize the character of the writing. Stein allows these ultimate linguistic shifters complete freedom. As a consequence, the nominal level of the texts is not determined "with reference to things," with reference to anything beyond the writing itself. In this sense one could describe the writing as "nonreferential." But the texts do not forbid one to supply "references"—on the contrary, in fact. Nonetheless the writing at every point emphasizes the fluid, arbitrary, and (in a philosophical sense) insubstantial nature of all references. As Stevens might say, they occur as they occur. The beauty of the writing is precisely a celebration—Stein's customary word is "pleasure"—of what is charming and evanescent.

In place of the substantiality of empirical phenomena, this writing proposes the substantiality of language. Stein's "language," however, is neither structure nor system; it is immediate usage, equal to nothing but itself. As we read we discern, in the reflective phases of our textual experience, the play of various abstract forms of language—semantic forms and syntactic forms, morphemes and phonemes. Punctuation is minimized to license the imagination of multiple forms, as many as possible. In Stein the system of language displays itself as a theater of verbal and literal figures. Because the emphasis upon immediacy is so strong, the texts seem nervous and alive. Stanzas in meditation indeed: thought as a process of thinking, thinking as a function of language, and language as the horizon within which human life goes on.

Had Milton been of our century, he might have called it not "darkness" but "language visible."

What the circulating library and the three-decker format did for nineteenth-century fiction, the Renaissance of Printing accomplished for twentieth-century writing, especially poetry. It supplied artists with a new horizon of bibliographical and institutional possibilities, and these brought with them many linguistic innovations as well. Some of the graphic experiments are dramatic—like "Bob" Brown's visual poems or the texts he collected in *Readies for Bob Brown's Machine* (1931). Djuna Barnes's haunting first volume, *Book of Repulsive Women* (1915), is a close marriage of her poetry and drawings. Even more intricate and effective is Laura Riding's pitiless satire of modernity *The Life of the Dead* (1933), a late collaborative work. John Aldridge's drawings are deeply woven into the writing of this poem—as deeply as the graphic features of Pound's first two book installments of the *Cantos* (1925, 1928).

More traditional writers (like Yeats and Stevens, for example) would exploit their new linguistic resources in relatively mild or derivative ways. This historical fact must not be taken to imply (as such) any value judgment on that work, only to describe its position with respect to the new linguistic materials. Most modernist writers did not break fresh ground but simply worked within the imaginative possibilities that had been opened for them. Riding's work, for example, is closely associated with the Seizen Press, the imprint she and Robert Graves created, principally as an outlet for her writing.

Functional as the material features of *The Life of the Dead* are (it was published by Arthur Barker Ltd.), Riding's Seizen Press books are just cleanly printed. Their language is not at all remarkably "visible." Yet even that plain printing style seems significant in its discretion, for it reflects Riding's growing preoccupation with linguistic clarity and simplicity.

The more romantic sorts of effect that Yeats achieved with his Dun Emer/Cuala Press formats have numerous analogues in modernist writing. Stevens, for example, liked to work with good printers, and certain of his books—*Ideas of Order* figures prominently here—cast the poems into significant material forms. The first edition was hand set at the Alcestis Press in an edition of 135 copies. Twenty copies are printed on Duca di Modena paper and the rest on Strathmore Permanent. In each case the paper is an arresting matte white, which throws the crisp dark print into sharp relief and gives the page an incised effect. The latter is dramatically enhanced by the typeface, named Inkunabula in the colophon, which imitates the uncial forms of early medieval manuscripts (see fig. 7). In Stevens's book it suggests an antique idea of order resisting all the "old chaos of the sun" and its transient inertias. The book design creates for the work as a whole a significant typographical environment, which then lies in wait, as it were, for peculiarly appropriate textual moments—as in the last lines of "The Reader":

> The sombre pages bore no print
> Except the trace of burning stars
> In the frosty heaven.

The final line of "The Circus Animals' Desertion" is analogous to this passage from Stevens. In each case we observe a special effect opportunistically seized. Both writers understood the importance of setting poems in a bibliographical field that would be able to enhance textual value in unpremeditated ways. There are graces available to writing when it gives its entire faith over to the greater resources of Language. Certain artists, however—Blake and Morris among them—are more active agents in those fields of grace. Blake's illuminated texts created, or revealed, forgotten possibilities of linguistic signification. The second coming of his work took place among the Pre-Raphaelites, whose devotion to materialities of expression sped the progress of the Renaissance of Printing.

THE READER

All night I sat reading a book,
Sat reading as if in a book
Of sombre pages.

It was autumn and falling stars
Covered the shrivelled forms
Crouched in the moonlight.

No lamp was burning as I read,
A voice was mumbling "Everything
Falls back to coldness,

Even the musky muscadines,
The melons, the vermilion pears
Of the leafless garden."

The sombre pages bore no print
Except the trace of burning stars
In the frosty heaven.

/ / / 43 / / /

7. Page from "To the Reader" in the first (Alcestis Press) edition of Wallace
Stevens's *Ideas of Order* (1935); Inkunabula typeface.

Emily Dickinson's career overlapped this period. Her refusal of print might be taken as a secret sign of her disinterest in the visibilities of language. But the opposite is the case. With the exception of Whitman, whose influence here would take many years to develop, American writers (and printers) did not attempt practical explorations of language's bibliographical resources for serious writing until the 1890s. Whatever explanations we favor for Dickinson's refusal of print, we must not let them obscure the deep interest she took in the visual aspects of her writing. Indeed, so radical was her work in this regard that one hundred years would pass before the true outlines of her textual innovations would appear in public. Certain people who had seen her manuscripts—most notably the poet Jack Spicer—recognized the truth beforehand, but their insights had no influence on the study of Dickinson.[25] The revelation came with the publication in 1981 of R. W. Franklin's edition of *The Manuscript Books of Emily Dickinson*.[26]

The first three volumes of Dickinson's poetry (1890, 1891, 1896), edited by Mabel Loomis Todd and Thomas Wentworth Higginson, have long stood as an emblem of well-intentioned but disastrous bowdlerization. The bibliographical character of these pale little volumes in fact deserves careful scrutiny, for they constructed an important and still influential frame for reading Dickinson's writing. Nevertheless, later readers (discovering the editorial changes made to Dickinson's poems by these texts) turned decisively away from them. A slow process of textual correction culminated in Thomas H. Johnson's important edition (1955) of *The Poems of Emily Dickinson*, where Johnson proposed to deliver as faithful a transcript of Dickinson's texts as a print medium could manage.[27] It was a thoughtful critical edition, with textual variants. Its chief (apparent) inadequacies were the numbering system, which encouraged a grotesque scholarly convention for referring to her poems, and the presentation of the writing as a long sequential poetic series. Johnson's arrangement was intended to counter the (equally but differently) misleading arrangement of the first editions, where the poems are given precious titles and collected into groups with Victorian ethico-religious headings: Book I.—Life; Book II.—Love; Book III.—Nature; Book IV.—Time and Eternity. Neither Johnson nor Todd and Higginson come close to reproducing Dickinson's own arrangement for her poems, which was quite distinctive. In the words of Mrs. Todd, the verses were gathered by the author into "over sixty little 'volumes,' each composed of four or five sheets of note paper tied together with twine."[28]

The principal object of Franklin's splendid 1981 edition was to reconstruct Dickinson's fascicles, which had been deconstructed by Todd and Higginson during their editing labors, and which had not been restored by Johnson. Franklin tried to supply readers—in facsimile—with something close to what the poet had actually left behind as her life's work. Scholarship has yet to assess the significance of Dickinson's fascicled arrangements as Franklin has reconstructed them. What his edition has done, however, is reveal new and more serious deficiencies in Johnson's (by now standard) typographical edition.[29]

Franklin's edition makes it clear that Dickinson's texts are what would later be called (by Charles Olson) "composition by field." The grouping of the poems into fascicles corresponds to a similar approach to the text at a more local level—a poetic deployment of writing within the given space of the page. Free verse forms are typically composed by field—the measure may be acoustical, visual, or some combination of the two. What is startling about Dickinson's work is that her field compositions are deployed within (a) verse conventions of simple metrical forms, typically the quatrain, and (b) certain scriptural/typographical conventions of text presentation.

Here is a simple example from a famous poem. The first text is Johnson's, the second attempts a more accurate typographical translation of Dickinson's actual writing.[30]

> Pain—has an Element of Blank—
> It cannot recollect
> When it begun—or if there were
> A time when it was not—   (no. 650, st. 1)
>
> Pain—has an Element
> of Blank—
> It cannot recollect
> When it began—or if
> there were
> A time when it was not

Even in this type-translation one observes how crucially *visible* this language is. The inertia of the quatrain supplies a subtextual measure for the play of variance. The most dramatic effects appear, I suppose, with the lines "of Blank—" and "When it began—or if." The first is a moment of what Pound would later call phanopoeia (Dickinson playing with the blank space created by her script), the second (which interrupts the quatrain measure to play with the logic of syntax) of logopoeia (see fig. 8).

It does no good to argue, as some might, that these odd lineations are unintentional—the result of Dickinson finding herself at the right edge of the page, and so folding her lines over. Her manuscripts show that she could preserve the integrity of the metrical unit if she wanted. Besides, certain textual moments reveal such a dramatic use of page space as to put the question of intentionality beyond consideration. "Pain—has an Element" supplies one such moment but many others might be offered—for example, from the poem customarily known as "Many a phrase has the English language" (Johnson, no. 276). I have particularly in mind the opening of the third quatrain (see fig. 9). Metrically considered the line unit is "Breaking in bright Orthography." When she comes to script this line, however, Dickinson writes:

> Breaking in bright Orthogra-
> > phy

She did not have to do this, her page had space for the whole of the metrical unit. The script is simply being turned into an emblem of itself. Needless to say, the Johnson text does not attempt to reproduce this important feature of Dickinson's poem.

Dickinson seems to have had a special fondness for dropping the last measure of a quatrain to a new (and separate) line; it is a characteristic feature of her scripts, as we see in both of the poems just mentioned as well as the following poem:

> Experience is the Angled
> Road
> Preferred against the
> Mind
> By—Paradox—The
> Mind itself
> Presuming it to lead
>
> Quite Opposite—How
> Complicate

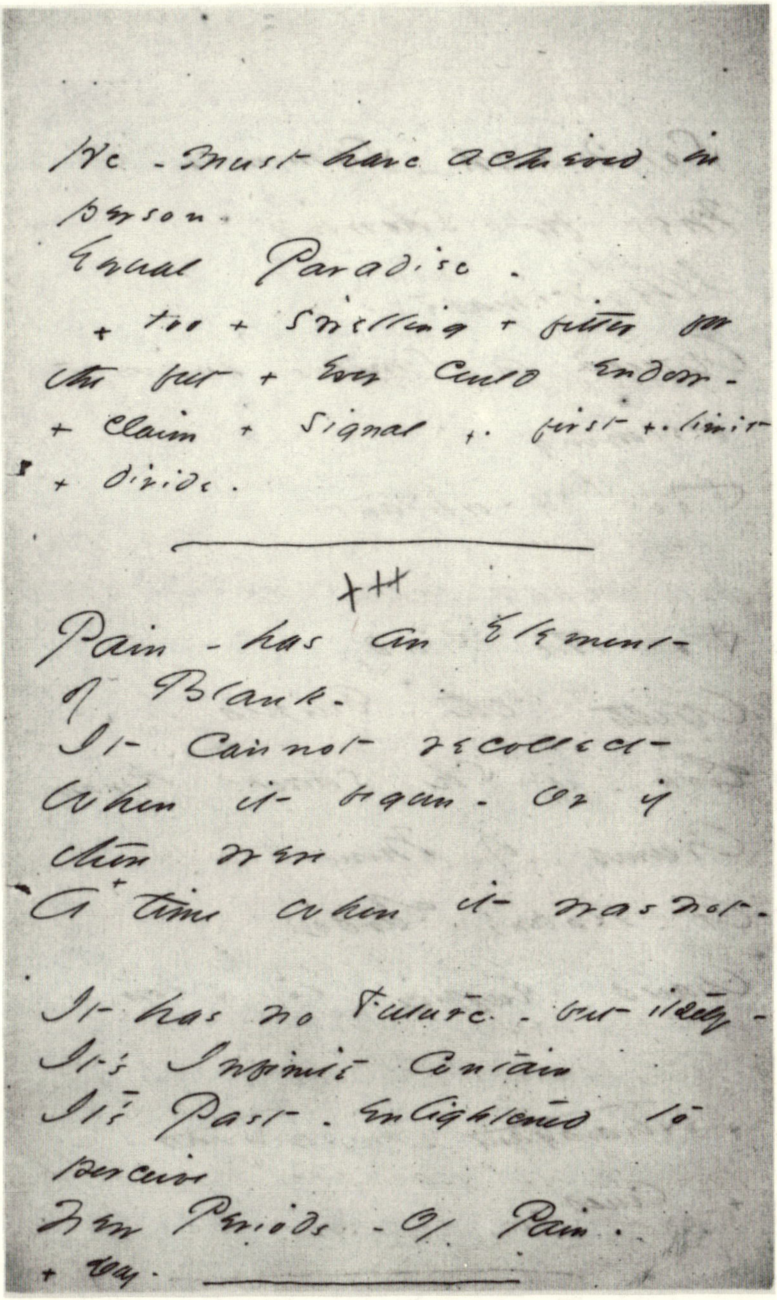
We - must have achieved in
person.
Equal Paradise.
+ too + Smiting + fitter for
… but + ever Could endow -
+ Claim + Signal + first + limit
+ divide.

Pain - has an Element -
of Blank -
It - Cannot recollect -
When it - began - Or if
there were
A time when it - was not -

It - has no Future - but itself -
It's Infinite Contain
It's Past - enlightened to
perceive
New Periods - Of Pain.
+ day.

8. Emily Dickinson, "Pain—has an Element," manuscript text.

9. Emily Dickinson, "Many a phrase has the," first page of the manuscript text.

The discipline of
Man—
Compelling him to
   Choose Himself
His Preappointed Pain—   (Johnson, no. 910)

When Johnson normalizes this poem into quatrains he destroys altogether one of its most important technical features: its repeated moves to isolate words and phrases, to fracture the traditional meter and syntax that serve as the basic subtext of the writing. Johnson's comment on his translation is interesting:

> The text is arranged as a single eight-line stanza. The sense of the poem is altered by the fact that the word "Paradox," intended to be used adverbially—(By—Paradox) *paradoxically*—is rendered substantively:

> Preferred against the mind
> By paradox, the mind itself
> Presuming it to lead
> Quite opposite.   (Johnson, II. 668–69)

The work is not, however, arranged as "a single eight-line stanza," not even in Johnson's sense: there is a distinct if small separation between lines 7 and 8 (Johnson's lines 4 and 5) (see fig. 10). The separation is important to see because it alludes to the quatrain subtext—which calls for a sharp separation here, were the text to be scripted in quatrains. Furthermore, the word "Paradox" is even more nervous than Johnson suggests, for it could serve at least two substantive functions: as object of the preposition (as Johnson suggests) or as simple exclamation.

The same kind of possibilities multiply through the text, most clearly in the final eight lines. By glossing only one of these "ambiguities," Johnson betrays no regard for the others. He does not see them, I suspect, because the text he chose to transcribe is not the text Dickinson wrote down. Her text—unlike Johnson's—has so loosened the hinges of its more formal subtext as to throw its words open to surprising linguistic possibilities. In the poetic form that Dickinson has scripted, these openings to alternative sense arrangements emerge principally because of the text's visual structure.

Dickinson's play with her text's graphic features is only beginning

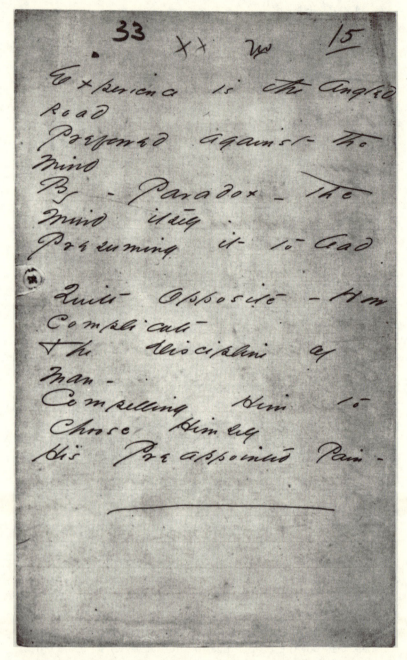

10. Emily Dickinson, "Experience is the Angled," manuscript text.

to be explored—principally by the poet Susan Howe and her student
Marta Werner. Howe, for example, has noted a pattern of important
effects that depend upon Dickinson's deployment of scriptural conventions for recording variant readings. Dickinson uses an "×"
(sometimes a "+")[31] to signal textual variants. Typically she arranges
these variants as a group at the conclusion of the poem, though the
variants can and do appear everywhere on the page, and not always
horizontally. In the face of these textual anomalies Johnson behaves
like a scholar wanting to bring conventional clarities to a writer's
idiosyncratic practices. He normalizes this material just as he normalizes Dickinson's metrical forms.

When Dickinson (I am describing here a typical procedure) puts
a superscript "+" or "×" at the head of a word or phrase, she invokes
a convention for signaling variant readings. Problems arise because
in Dickinson's texts the scholar's notational system for marking the
relations between a "superior text" and its "variants" is not clearly
preserved. What happens is difficult to describe abstractly or in general. The case of "Those fair fictitious People" (Johnson, no. 499)
may serve to illustrate the textual possibilities (see fig. 11). Searching
this labyrinth Johnson carefully separates out a set of textual variants
to which he gives specific line numbers and lemmas. Another scholar
might have distinguished interlinear from terminal variants, and
might also have suggested—given the line drawn near the bottom of
the second page after the first set of terminal variants—that Dickinson wrote out a later (second or third) level of variance. In this imagination of the text, the late variants would be the final sequence

> × fingers. × Everlasting Childhood—
> Where are They—Can you tell—

The problem is that Dickinson's texts resist the orderliness
Johnson wants to construct. Johnson's lists of variants are often
nothing more than editorial surmises that ignore manifest anomalies
(here, for instance, Dickinson has placed a superscript "×" before the
word "Beyond" [line 12; Johnson's line 11], but Johnson's list gives no
variant for the word). Furthermore, because Dickinson places most
of the "variants" at the end, in a kind of block grouping with no cue
to lineation, it is difficult to read them scholastically—here in particular, because the poem covers two sides of a single sheet. As a consequence, in Dickinson's texts these "variant" materials tend to occupy

11. Emily Dickinson, "Those fair—fictitious People—," manuscript text (two pages).

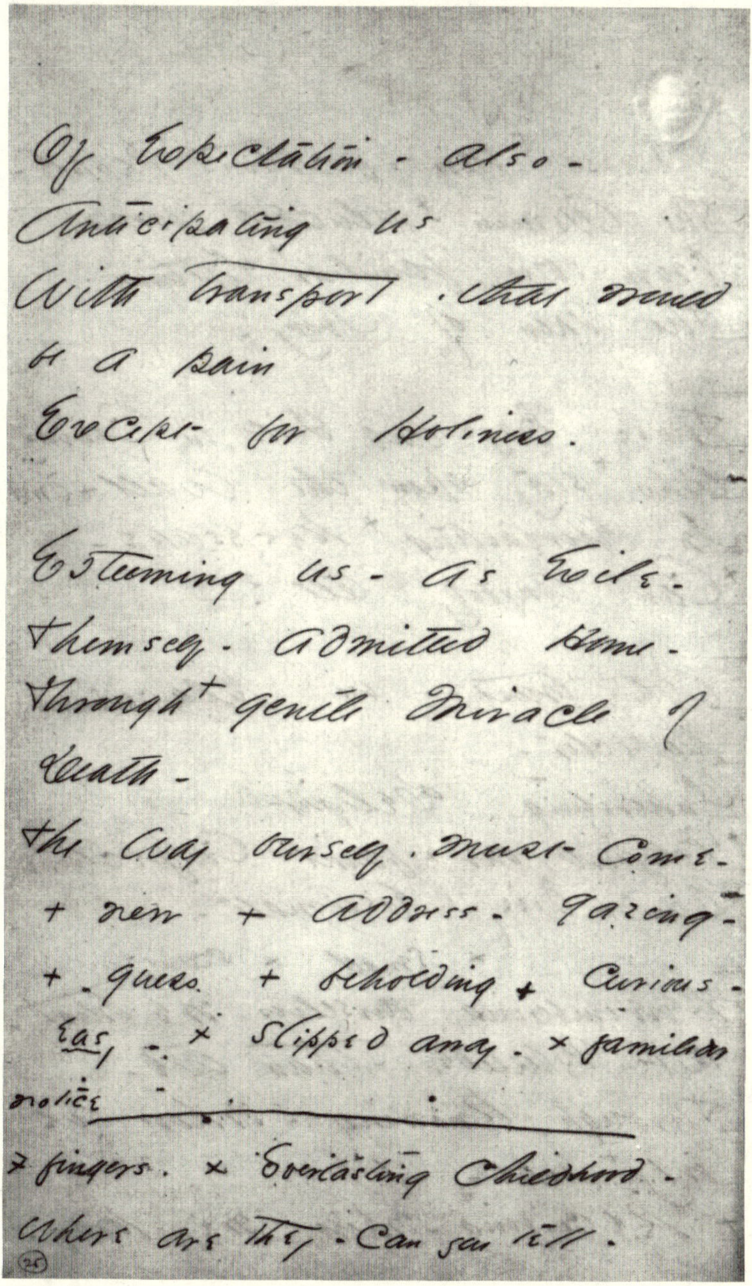
Of Expectation - also -
Anticipating us
With transport, that would
be a pain
Except for Holiness.

Esteeming us - as Exile -
Themself - admitted Home -
Through+ gentle Miracle of
Death -
The Way ourself, must come -
+ new + address - gazing -
+ guess + beholding + Curious -
Ear, - + slipped away - + familiar
notice
+ fingers - + Everlasting Childhood -
Where are they - Can you tell -
25

a kind of free space, further airing out a text that is being loosened in the ways I discussed earlier. In this textual situation, the final list of variants comes to the eye as a textual coda—the equivalent, for the poem as a whole, of a "feminine ending" (see the final two "variant lines" quoted above).

A brief poem like "Departed—to the Judgment" (Johnson, no. 524) gives a clear—perhaps a too clear—general illustration of the basic Dickinson schema (see also fig. 12).

> Departed—to the Judgment—
> A Mighty—Afternoon—
> Great Clouds—like Ushers—
> ×leaning—
> Creation—looking on—
>
> The Flesh—Surrendered—
> ×Cancelled—
> The Bodiless—begun—
> ×Two Worlds—like Audiences—
> ×dispense—
> And leave the Soul—alone—
>
> × placing × shifted × the—
> × dissolve—withdraw—retire—

As here, Dickinson's variants haunt the mind with insinuations. One *sees* the conventional relations signaled by the "×s," but the writing draws one away from those normalities to encourage a freer way with the text. More than a set of "variants" for the poem's two "stanzas," the words appear also as an unrhymed couplet of verbal shards—as it were the poem's final, collapsing gloss on itself. (To read this work aloud—taking the lineation and dashes as cues for an oral pacing— can help to educate our eyes to a more liberated scholarly vision of how language is being used here.)

One last example where the final "variants" seem to carry the poem away at the end: "I took my Power in my Hand" (Johnson, no. 540):

> I took my Power in my Hand—
> And went against the
> World—

12. Emily Dickinson, "Departed—to the Judgment—," manuscript text.

'Twas not so much as
David–had–
But I–was twice as bold–

I aimed my Pebble–but
Myself
Was all the one that fell—
Was it Goliah–was too
large–
Or⁺ was myself–too small?
⁺ just myself—Only me–I– (See fig. 13.)

Johnson's editorial treatment of this text once again normalizes the
"quatrains" and separates the variants into a scholar's apparatus. It
clearly alters the original scriptural version in drastic ways. The last
line of Dickinson's text—that is to say, the line of "variants"—undergoes the greatest change from this intervention. Reading those
words as an apparatus or as the poem's concluding line—as one or
the other or both—makes all the difference in the world.

Johnson's edition goes astray—misrepresents Dickinson's writing—because it has approached her work as if it aspired to a typographical existence. On the contrary, Dickinson's scripts cannot be
read as if they were "printer's copy" manuscripts, or as if they were
composed with an eye toward some state beyond their handcrafted
textual condition. Her surviving manuscript texts urge us to take
them at face value, to treat all her scriptural forms as potentially
significant *at the aesthetic or expressive level*. Calligraphic variations
have to be carefully scrutinized, the same way we scrutinize all poetry
for lexical nuances at the linguistic level. Some of her scripts are
highly ornamental, some are not, and we must attend to these variant
features of the texts. In the same way we have to read closely the
lineation patterns, and the spacing of the scripts at every level, as well
as the choice of papers and other writing materials. In a poetry that
has imagined and executed itself as a scriptural rather than a typographical event, all these matters fall under the work's initial horizon
of finality. Emily Dickinson's poetry was not written *for* a print medium, even though it was written *in* an age of print. When we come
to edit her work for bookish presentation, therefore, we must accommodate our typographical conventions to her work, not the other
way round.

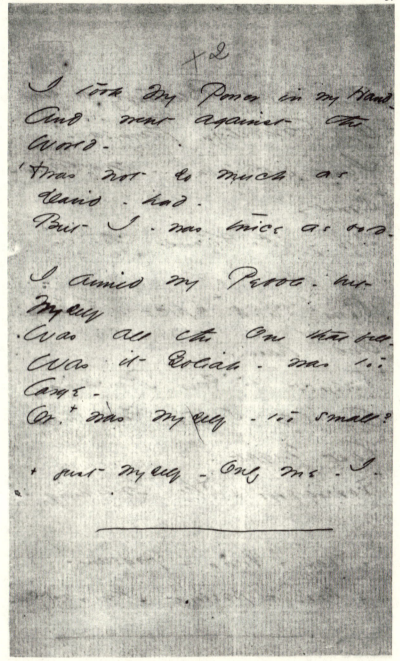

13. Emily Dickinson, "I took My Power in my Hand—," manuscript text.

❦

As with the reception history of Blake, the printing history of Dickinson's writing testifies to the historically advanced character of her work. Of Todd and Higginson's edition Johnson has correctly observed:

> The principles that guided Mrs. Todd and Col. Higginson in their editorial procedure were those that he had laid down, and they were dictated largely by standards of current literary taste. Thus the alterations which occur in the three series of *Poems* were deliberate and conscientiously made in an effort, however misguided it seems in retrospect, to give the poetry of Emily Dickinson the sort of finish which the sensibilities of the time were thought to demand. (Johnson, I. xliii)

From our "retrospect," however, this paragraph could be applied exactly to Johnson's work. If the Todd and Higginson edition seems a pure product of nineteenth-century America, Johnson's is an excellent example of a scholar's New Critical edition. To say this is not at all to argue, or even to suggest, that either of those editions are "bad" or uselessly out of date (or even, as Johnson said of Todd and Higginson's edition, "misguided"). Both seem to me indispensable for anyone wanting to understand either Dickinson's writing or its relation to the historical development of the language of culture during the past two hundred years.

Franklin's edition is much closer to the linguistic interests of a period that has seen the emergence in the past twenty years of "genetic" texts and editing procedures. Franklin is not himself such an editor, and his work acquires its significance by seizing the privilege of its historical backwardness. That is to say, Franklin's facsimile edition, which is technically precritical, puts the reader in closer touch with Dickinson's original scene of writing. That kind of textual access has been much valued during the past twenty years.

It has been said—by Foucault and others of our time—that literature crossed a threshold when it began to be read not as a set of works but as a scene of writing. Foucault traced this event to Flaubert but many other tracings have been made—to Rousseau, to Blake, whatever. The dawn is differently—*in*differently—red. Beyond question, however, is the fact of a threshold event. One of its unmistakable signals was the late nineteenth-century's Renaissance of Printing, whose practical influence on imaginative writing will be sketched in the first part of this book. Less easy to judge, though it can be far more absorbing, is the significance of the historical events for writing and reading. In the second part I try to suggest a way of thinking about that significance.

▓ PART ONE

A Revolution of the Word

It was written when all the world was going crazy about typographic form.

—William Carlos Williams on *Spring and All* (1923), in *I Wanted to Write a Poem* (1958)

1

"Thing to Mind": The Materialist Aesthetic of William Morris

PERHAPS because poetry descends to us through an early tradition of recitation and performance, poets set a high value on the integration of medium and message. In an ideal relation, form and content interact completely, as Yeats argued when he imagined the fusion of the dancer and the dance.

Yeats applied that figure of an integral art to a specifically poetic ideal; and he did so because he knew how difficult the ideal had become for the practicing poet. In a social environment dominated by typographical media and publishing institutions, poets no longer stand in the same immediate relation to their work as the dancer might be imagined to stand. A physical gap has opened between the poet and the execution of the poem. From Yeats's perspective at the beginning of the twentieth century, the gap had become an institutionalized gulf.

The work of William Morris, like that of Blake and Dickinson, seems to me most significant as an effort to come to grips with this problem of poetry's relation to its material encoding. In Morris's view the problem had become especially acute about four hundred years earlier, when the scriptural tradition began to pass over into the age of print. So long as printing and bookmaking were skilled crafts carried out in a culture of artisanal practices, the problem was, according to Morris, a manageable one. But processes of mechanization developed rapidly, and poets had increasingly to accommodate the production and distribution of their work to persons and institutions whose interests were primarily commercial.

All this is a familiar tale, as is Morris's famous response to the crisis he perceived. His involvement in the Arts and Crafts movement, his founding of Morris and Co. and the Kelmscott Press, climaxed an artistic career whose impact on the art and culture of the twentieth century is not easy to calculate. It is an influence that has also been generally misunderstood. A key feature of all Morris's work is its "quoted" or secondary status. The fabrics, the furniture, the books, the pictures, the poetry: by coming forward explicitly as imitations, all this work announced itself as what modernism would later call "constructivist." In every case the fundamental subject is the craft and the art of the making which is brought to one's attention through the work-as-imitation.

So far as poetry is concerned, Morris's work is at once extremely concrete and extremely reflexive. The poetry calls attention to every feature and level of its construction. When Morris writes a literary ballad, as we shall see, the "literariness" of the work operates as a second-order convention. The convention of "the literary" highlights the material features (morphemic and phonemic) of poetic language as we have received them through a first-order set of (ballad) conventions. Morris's work is therefore properly to be called "aesthetic" (or "primitive" or "naive") because its subject is poetry itself—or more particularly, poetry as it may be carried out in an age of capitalist mechanical reproduction.

His literary work thus comes forward under the Goethean sign "in the beginning was the deed," rather than the Judeo-Christian sign "in the beginning was the word." In this respect we judge one of Morris's greatest insights to have been the understanding that no distinction should be permitted between the conception of the poem and the conception of the text. For Morris, when composition (in every sense) begins, inspiration must not be permitted to wane in the least way.

Morris worked to integrate the poem and its performative medium not by seeking a return to oral traditions of production, but by acknowledging the compositional environment as a necessary condition for the creation of modern poetry. Of course part of his acknowledgment called for acts of resistance against current printing and publishing practices. But as with Dickinson and Blake, those resistances were carried out as part of a broad-scale effort to exploit as completely as possible all the resources of the physical media that were the vehicular forms of his writing. How he did this is what I wish to talk about here.

※

Even at the start of his career, when he scarcely realized what might be accomplished along these lines, Morris sent a clear typographical signal of his imaginative intentions. This appears as the printer's imprint on the decorated green wrappers covering each of the twelve issues of *The Oxford and Cambridge Magazine* (1856), and also at the end of Morris's first book of poetry, *The Defence of Guenevere, and Other Poems* (1858). Both works were published by Bell and Daldy, who often used Chiswick Press in the books they issued. In the magazine the imprint reads simply "printed by C. Whittingham, Tooks Court, Chancery Lane." The book of poetry sets the equivalent imprint at the foot of the last printed page, where it reads (more particularly): "Chiswick Press:—Printed by C. Whittingham, Tooks Court, Chancery Lane."[1]

Of course many give little or no attention to these kinds of bibliographical notations, which can seem irrelevant to the literary or imaginative character of writing. But those imprints tell the reader a great deal about Morris's first publications. First and most important, they tell us that the physical appearance of these works had been given serious thought, and that a conscious decision had been made to put the printing of these texts into the hands of one of the few fine-printing houses then operating in England.[2]

We know that Morris underwrote the cost of his first book of poetry and that he bore virtually the entire expense of the magazine as well.[3] It is not clear, at this date, whether he and his friends chose Bell and Daldy as the publisher for their new magazine because the firm often used Chiswick Press as their printer, which in fact Bell and Daldy did; or if they chose Chiswick Press, and then went with the publisher Bell and Daldy at the printer's suggestion. Morris's financial investment in *The Oxford and Cambridge Magazine* would have given him and his friends authority to name their printer. In either case, Morris was involved in a deliberate effort to see that Chiswick Press would print these early works.

What is important to realize is that few writers in the mid-1850s would have given any thought to such matters, or would have known that fine-printing traditions had been established and maintained at Chiswick Press during one of the worst periods of the English book trade. Many nineteenth-century writers published books at their own expense, of course, especially at the outset of their writing careers. Very few who did saw their financial interest in such publishing ventures as an imaginative opportunity. Morris did, so that his first published works exhibit their artistic aims in the most material and apparent way—at the level of the books' bibliographical codes.

The Oxford and Cambridge Magazine and *The Defence of Guenevere* volumes are both printed in a typical Chiswick Press style. The typeface is their familiar modern Caslon neatly printed, the same font used by William Pickering and (later) Bell and Daldy in their editions of the famous Aldine Poets series.[4] In the magazine the printing is in close double columns, whereas in the collection of poems the lines are more generously leaded. Simplicity and clarity dominate the printed page. It is this clean typographical style that provides such an excellent context for the decorated capitals and headpiece ornaments in both books, and for the other ornamental devices which appear at various moments in *The Defence of Guenevere* volume.

The fact that both of these early books are printed in a modern face Caslon needs some comment. Morris's early books are unusual for the way they have mixed together features of two distinctive Chiswick Press styles. The two styles are epitomized by, on one hand, the Aldine Poets volumes, which are printed in a modern Caslon without ornaments or decorated capitals; and, on the other, those books which the press began to issue in the mid-1840s such as *The Diary of Lady Willoughby* (1844) and Herbert's *The Temple* (1850). The latter are printed with ornaments, decorated capitals, and in the remarkable old face Caslon font, with its distinctive long "s." Unlike the press's Aldine Poets volumes, *The Oxford and Cambridge Magazine* and *The Defence of Guenevere* both carry various ornaments and decorated initials. Their texts, however, are printed in modern face rather than old face.

Morris's mixed page layout indicates that his interest in typography was initially focused on the ornamental features of the text rather than on the typeface. That interest is borne out by Morris's typographical experiments of the 1870s, when he tried—with Burne-Jones—to invent a new kind of book: the abortive experiments with highly decorative editions of *The Earthly Paradise* and *Love is Enough*.

I shall have more to say about Morris's involvement with books and printing. At this point, however, I want to reflect on the relation between Morris's interest in the physique of books and the purely linguistic aspects of his early poetical work. This relation is important to establish because it helps us to understand Morris's peculiar and highly innovative understanding of poetry and poetical form. *The Defence of Guenevere* volume, the unique *A Book of Verse* which

Morris wrote and illuminated in 1870 as a birthday present for Georgiana Burne-Jones, and the late *Poems by the Way*, the second book issued by the Kelmscott Press (in 1891), are in an important sense three distinctive ways which Morris found for expressing his new vision of poetical form. Although the physical composition of the three books is very different, each calls our attention to poetry as a materially-oriented act of imagination. In them "meaning" is most fully constituted not as a conception but as an embodiment.

The famous Pre-Raphaelite attention to minute detail is of course our best index to Morris's vision of poetry as language incarnate. In prose and poetry alike Morris forces the reader into a verbal environment that is so thick and dense as to stagger the irresolute imagination. "The Story of the Unknown Church," which Morris published in the first issue of *The Oxford and Cambridge Magazine*, supplies numerous typical examples:

> The Abbey where we built the Church was not girt by stone walls, but by a circle of poplar trees, and whenever a wind passed over them, were it ever so little a breath, it set them all a-ripple; and when the wind was high, they bowed and swayed very low, and the wind, as it lifted the leaves, and showed their silvery white sides, or as again in the lulls of it, it let them drop, kept on changing the trees from green to white, and white to green; moreover, through the boughs and trunks of the poplars, we caught glimpses of the great corn sea, waving, waving, waving, for leagues and leagues; and among the corn grew burning scarlet poppies, and blue cornflowers. . . .

> Then farther from the Church, and past the cloister and its buildings, were many detached buildings, and a great garden round them, all within the circle of the poplar trees; in the garden were trellises covered over with roses, and convolvulus, and the great-leaved fiery nasturtium; and specially all along by the poplar trees were there trellises, but on these grew nothing but deep crimson roses; the hollyhocks too were all out in blossom at that time, great spires of pink, and orange, and red, and white, with their soft downy leaves.[5]

It is as if, in reading passages like these that describe such common and familiar things, one were being led to a recovery of the powers of vision, to see again for the first time. The text's attentiveness, so coolly represented, seems for that reason all the more startling—paradoxically unnatural even in its descriptions from nature, almost unreal.

In fact, the narrator of this story (we learn in the last sentence) is dead, so that his narrative and descriptions are imagined as coming to us from another world. Extraordinary acuity, in Morris's texts, always depends upon some similar kind of alienation effect by which we are able, as Morris once so famously wrote, to "forget six counties overhung with smoke." So Morris will frequently position his text in a reverie or dream environment because, as the narrator of this story says, "In my dream I could see even very far off things much clearer than we see real material things on the earth."[6]

The Pre-Raphaelite effect emerges as a translation of the familiar into the strange. From the reader's vantage, the style comes as a kind of benevolent reproach. It tells us that though we live in the world, we commonly do not see the smallest part of its material particularity, which for Morris is its wondrousness.

The effect is more arresting still when it is executed in a poetical context like *The Defence of Guenevere* volume. The poem "Golden Wings," for example, begins with the description of a castle that recalls the Church described in "The Story of the Unknown Church."

> Midways of a walled garden,
>   In the happy poplar land,
>   Did an ancient castle stand,
> With an old knight for a warden.
>
> Many scarlet bricks there were
>   In its walls, and old grey stone;
>   Over which red apples shone
> At the right time of the year.   (1–8)

Here words and phrases acquire a kind of incised particularity. "Scarlet bricks" are not merely set off against "grey stone," they stand out as well because of the differential summoned by the phrase "red apples." This text invites us to ponder, or perhaps imagine, a precise difference between "scarlet" and "red"; and that invitation defines the style of the text as a whole. When we finish the poem, phrases like "an old knight for a warden" and "the right time of the year" will haunt the mind because they will have been given an immediate and purely textual life. That warden has no part to play in the narrative of the poem—he is as it were a free particular, a poetical gift, a grace note. As for "the right time of the year," it might be translated, because of its association in the poem with love, as "spring"; but in fact the poem forbids any translation, insisting instead that the phrase be equal to nothing but itself. This "right time" might be any time of any year,[7] for in this poetical place

> there was a boat
> Of carven wood, with hangings green
> About the stern; it was great bliss
> For lovers to sit there and kiss
> In the hot summer noons, not seen.   (16–20)

The ballad genre is exactly right for the kind of effect Morris wants to secure. It is an iconic genre of framed events, brief scenes, and formulaic language. The ballad's linguistic features are especially effective in the latter-day context of the nineteenth century because they force our attention to fall on what might otherwise seem trivial details. The word "Did" in the third line of "Golden Wings," for example, quoted earlier, is placed in such a strong textual position that we notice it even though it seems of no special thematic consequence. The phrase "there were," situated in the important rhyme position of the fifth line, similarly calls attention to itself. The two words in the phrase might as easily be reversed, of course, since the lexical meaning would remain the same and the off-rhyme would still be secured (instead of "were/year" we would have "there/year"). This unrealized textual possibility would turn the word "there" into an adverb of place. As it is, because the word hovers between adverb and dummy subject, the reader must linger with the phrase, and glimpse a nominal latency in an adverb, and a concrete meaning in the normally empty expletive "there."

The poetical *point* in both cases is exactly to force us to pay attention to these small words. In the aesthetic of this verse, the poem's desire to renovate vision cannot be successful if it does not succeed to waken our attention to the (apparently) least remarkable features of the text. We observe this aesthetic of observation throughout the poem (and the volume as a whole)—for example, in the following passage:

> Across the moat the fresh west wind
>   In very little ripples went;
>   The way the heavy aspens bent
> Towards it, was a thing to mind.   (21–24)

Here sound and rhythm are everything. A phrase like "very little" works so well partly because it brings a word like "very," corpsed and eviscerated by everyday inattention, back to life again.

This particular stanza is also quite interesting for its final line, where the poem explicitly introduces a mental category of value into the text's purely sensory, material, and aesthetic environment. We note that the "mind" invoked here is not the rational or even the hermeneutical mind. Rather, it is a mind that works simply by paying attention to things, by marking scenes, effects, impressions. This mind is to register the exact way these trees bend and this water ripples; it is to note the kind of trees and the direction of the wind; it is to note—as we saw in the texts cited earlier—the colors and textures and physique of things. This is the mind of sensation and experience, the mind—in brief—of lovers whose emblematic condition is "to sit there and kiss / In the hot summer noons, not seen."

But where *is* "there," where are these unseen kissing lovers, these beings devoted to a life of sensations rather than a life of thoughts? This question is explicitly posed in a poem like "The Tune of Seven Towers."

> No one goes there now:
>   For what is left to fetch away
> From the desolate battlements all arow,
>   And the lead roof heavy and grey?
> *"Therefore," said fair Yolande of the flowers,*
> *"This is the tune of Seven Towers."*
>
> No one walks there now;
>   Except in the white moonlight
> The white ghosts walk in a row;
>   If one could see it, an awful sight,—
> *"Listen!" said fair Yolande of the flowers,*
> *"This is the tune of Seven Towers."*
>
> But none can see them now,
>   Though they sit by the side of the moat,

Feet half in the water, there in a row,
　　Long hair in the wind afloat.
"Therefore," said fair Yolande of the flowers,
"This is the tune of Seven Towers."

If any will go to it now,
　　He must go to it all alone,
Its gates will not open to any row
　　Of glittering spears—will *you* go alone?
"Listen!" said fair Yolande of the flowers,
"This is the tune of Seven Towers."　　　　　(1–24)

❀ Don't these poems you keep quoting strike you as quaint, even museum pieces? I mean, our principal subject *is* modernism, isn't it? To a modernist eye and ear these texts seem to come from another (dreamy) world.

Yeats and Pound (among others) took them as their points of departure, didn't they?

❀ Yes of course, but only in their hot youth, as it were. Virtually everything they achieved *as* modernists left this type of soft late romanticism behind.

Perhaps the problem lies not with these texts, so important for Yeats and Pound, but with the habits of reading we have academically acquired. None of these works by Morris strike me as "soft" in the least. Compared with the ballads of the romantic period as such, Morris's *Defence of Guenevere* poems represent new departures because they want to incise and harden the edges of their signifiers.

Nor is the pursuit of exactitude simply a matter of ornamental clarity. "The Tune of Seven Towers," for example, poses a riddle and a test for the "*you*" addressed in the last quoted stanza. To solve the puzzle and meet the test this "*you*" must go "there," to the place associated with the Seven Towers, which is now inhabited only by ghostly lovers. When we realize that the poem itself comprises seven stanzas, and that the second line of the refrain is entirely self-reflexive, the riddle of the text becomes clear. The poem is a game of words addressed to the reader, who may "By my love go there now" (25) if he chooses to do so.[8] The phrase "my love" is, like everything else in this work, a purely textual condition—something which we might translate, anthropomorphically, as the poem's desire for the reader.

Morris locates "there" as a textual condition in the marvellous wit playing in the first word of the refrain. The word "*Therefore*" enters the poem with that abrupt illogic so characteristic of the ballad inheritance. Commonplace meaning expects the word to establish a cause/effect syntax, but of course no such syntax emerges. By stripping the word of its commonplace meaning Morris tempts and tests the reader (the "*you*" of line 22) to locate a different meaning in "*Therefore*." And suddenly it appears at the poem's lexical and phonemic (as opposed to its semantic and referential) levels—as the internal rhyme linked to the key word "there" that came be*fore* in the first line.

"*Therefore . . . This is*": these words standing at the head of the two refrain lines sum up the self-reflexive game being played out in this work. The hermeneutical mind might happily dwell for some time with those small words, teasing out deep meanings from them. For Morris, however, that procedure, while a certain pleasure in itself, is not essential. What is required is a more material action of the mind. For this is a poetry of experience of an even more direct and intense order than Browning's, to whom, indeed, Morris was deeply in debt from the start of his career.

So where is "there" with its unseen kissing lovers, its white ghosts, its golden wings? It is a textual place where the imagination recovers its material life. Finally we have to say that it is Morris's poetry itself. Most emphatically is it not in the world of the six counties overhung with smoke. By the measures (in both senses) of Morris's texts, the people in the six counties are unalive, immaterial, unreal. Living under the rule of the commercial and managing men of that world, they are textually located in the "*you*" addressed and challenged by "*fair Yolande of the flowers*." They might, according to Morris, find their lives again by regaining contact with that fuller and more humanly material condition glimpsed in the simple, but finally enriched, phrase "*This is*." Morris intends his poems as a vehicle for bringing about that secular resurrection of the dead. For such persons the way back to experience is imagined to lie, paradoxically, through the textual condition.

The importance of that condition, for Morris as for Blake before him, is that it forces us to attend to and question the appearances of things. What, for example, is the defense of the sinful Queen Guenevere? She argues that it is appearance itself, the beauty of her particular being. But what is that being? At first it seems her bodily loveliness, nor is that aspect of her beauty ever irrelevant. But if we shift the scale of our attention slightly, we see that her defense lies as well, like Sheharazade's, in her words, in the text she spins out as she seeks to hold off the impending doom of an arbitrary and self-serving moral code. And if we shift the scale again we see that her ultimate defense is the poetical work of "The Defence of Guenevere," the title poem in a book of verse headed by the same title.

Imagining poetry in this way, Morris was in an important sense obliged in conscience to secure the Chiswick Press, or its equivalent, to print his book. His own "defense" of Guenevere could not be raised—at any rate would be weakened as a defense—if he neglected this aspect of his work's beauty, this form of its rhetoric.

Remarkable as this early book is, it scarcely began the realization of Morris's imaginative ideals. *The Defence of Guenevere* volume largely operates at its linguistic level alone. It is true that the materiality of the book and its texts does not positively interfere with the language of the work. *The Defence of Guenevere and Other Poems* is neither an ugly nor an indifferently printed book (see fig. 14). Nevertheless, the poems do not substantially exploit the bibliographical resources of their textuality. Indeed, those resources were relatively meager ones, even when they were supplied by the Chiswick Press. Morris embarked on the abortive "book that never was,"[9] the great ornamented text of *The Earthly Paradise*, precisely because—by the late 1860s—he had begun to realize what poetry might be able to do for itself by forcing the graphics of print technology to work in and with the language of the poems.

Morris had to abandon the great *Earthly Paradise* project as too massive, too expensive—finally, in fact, beyond the resources that he was able to command, or that even the Chiswick Press could supply. As many have remarked, a crucial deficiency lay in the typefaces available to him at the time. Trial pages for the ornamented *Earthly Paradise* were set at Chiswick Press, some in old-face Caslon, some in a more substantial Basle.[10] The decorative materials overwhelmed the typefaces, however, and made the pages appear to crumble under their own weight. The same thing happened when Morris attempted, in 1872, an elaborately ornamented edition of *Love is Enough* (see figs. 15 and 16).

THE TUNE OF SEVEN TOWERS.

O one goes there now :
    For what is left to fetch away
  From the desolate battlements all arow,
    And the lead roof heavy and grey ?
" *Therefore,*" *said fair Yoland of the flowers,*
" *This is the tune of Seven Towers.*"

  No one walks there now ;
    Except in the white moonlight
  The white ghosts walk in a row ;
    If one could see it, an awful sight,—
" *Listen !*" *said fair Yoland of the flowers,*
" *This is the tune of Seven Towers.*"

  But none can see them now,
    Though they sit by the side of the moat,

14. William Morris, "The Tune of Seven Towers," from *The Defence of Guenevere and Other Poems* (1858 edition).

The Story of Cupid and Psyche.

Argument.

Psyche was a King's daughter, whose beauty made all people forget Venus, wherefore the Goddess hated her, and would fain have destroyed her: nevertheless she became the bride of Love, but her sisters gave her such evil counsel that he was wrath with her, and left her: wherein, she, having first revenged herself of her sisters, wandered the world seeking him, and so doing, fell into the hands of Venus, who tormented her, and set her fearful tasks to accomplish; but the Gods and all nature helped her, so that at last she was reunited to love, forgiven by Venus, and made immortal by the Father of Gods and Men.

Part I.

I N the Greek land of old there was
a King [thing,
Happy in battle, rich in every
But chiefly that he had a young
daughter [in her,
Who was so fair all men rejoiced

Psyche and her beauty.

So fair that strangers, landed from the sea,
Beholding her, thought verily that she
Was Venus visible to mortal eyes,
Fresh come from Cyprus for a world's surprise.
She was so beautiful, that had she stood
On windy Ida by the oaken-wood,
And bared her body to that shepherd's gaze,
Troy might have stood till now with happy days,
And those three fairest all have gone away
And left her with the apple on that day.

And Psyche is her name in stories old
As even by our fathers we were told;
All this saw Venus from her golden throne,
And knew that she no longer was alone

Psyche hated of Venus.

For beauty, but, if even for a while
This damsel matched her God-enticing smile:
Wherefore she wrought in such a wife, that she,
If honoured as a Goddess, certainly,

Was dreaded as a Goddess none the less,
And pined away long time in loneliness.
Two sisters had she, and men called them fair—
But as king's daughters might be anywhere,—
And these to lords of great name and estate
Were wedded, but at home must Psyche wait.

Her sisters wedded, but she a virgin.

The sons of kings before her silver feet
Still bowed and sighed for her; in music sweet
The minstrels to all men still sung her praise,
While she must live a virgin all her days.

So to Apollo's temple sent the King
To ask for aid and counsell in this thing,
And therewith sent he goodly gifts of price,
A silken veil wrought with a paradise,
Three golden bowls set round with many a gem,
Three silver cloaks, gold sewn in every hem,
And a fair ivory image of the God
That underfoot a golden serpent trod:
And when three lords with these were gone away
And must be gone won till the twentieth day,
Ill was the King at ease, and neither took
Joy in the chase, nor in the pictured book
The skilled Athenian limner had just wrought,
Or in the golden cloths from India brought,
At last the day came for those lords' return,

The King sends to the oracle.

15. William Morris, "The Story of Cupid and Psyche," proof sheet for aborted early edition of *The Earthly Paradise.*

LOVE IS ENOUGH.   5

THE MUSIC.

*L*OVE *is enough: though the world be*
a-waning,
And the woods have no voice but the voice
of complaining;
Though the sky be too dark for dim
eyes to discover
The gold-cups and daisies fair blooming
thereunder,
Though the hill be held shadows, and the
sea a dark wonder,
And this day draw a veil over all deeds passed over,
Yet their hands shall not tremble, their feet shall not falter;
The void shall not weary, the fear shall not alter
These lips and these eyes of the loved and the lover.

THE EMPEROR.

The spears flashed by me, and the spears swept round,
And in war's hopeless tangle was I bound,
But straw and stubble were the cold points found,
For still thy hands led down the weary way.

THE EMPRESS.

Through hall and street they led me as a queen,
They looked to see me proud and cold of mien,
I heeded not though all my tears were seen,
For still I dreamed of thee throughout the day.

16. William Morris, *Love is Enough*, proof sheet for aborted edition.

In each of these cases Morris finally decided to publish his poetry without the elaborate decorative features he was experimenting with. The necessary typefaces, to Morris's mind, were simply not there. In any case, as Morris would later observe in his 1893 lecture "The Ideal Book,"

> Whatever the subject-matter of the book may be, and however bare it may be of decoration, it can still be a work of art, if the type be good and attention be paid to its general arrangement.[11]

Chiswick Press was important for Morris because its work showed that these general principles, so brilliantly inaugurated in the fifteenth century, could still be followed in the nineteenth. Not until 1888, however, four years after Morris began his close connection with the typographer Emery Walker, would a final breakthrough to a great work like *Poems by the Way*, set in Golden type, become feasible.

But if the collaborative *Earthly Paradise* and *Love is Enough* were both abandoned, Morris did produce at that time one of his most extraordinary books of poetry, the unique illuminated work he titled simply *A Book of Verse* (1870). This understated title conceals an important allusion to a text from the first edition of Fitzgerald's *Rubaiyat*:

> Here with a Loaf of Bread beneath the Bough,
> A Flask of Wine, a Book of Verse—and Thou
>   Beside me singing in the Wilderness—
> And Wilderness is Paradise enow.

The allusion is apt for a book which, as Philip Henderson has remarked, was made as "a token of his love for Georgiana Burne-Jones."[12] But personal as this work is—its unique status takes, in this regard, its exact measure—the book equally stands as the first complete example of the poetical ideal Morris was striving after.

That is to say, the book has imagined a total integration of all its textual elements. The words and the verse forms, the calligraphy, decorative work, coloring, and page design: all have been imagined collectively together. The verse is by Morris, as is the calligraphy, the general design, and much of the coloring and other decorative work. The title page is therefore properly headed "A Book of Verse/ by/ William Morris/ Written in London/ 1870" and properly carries a small portrait of Morris. But the portrait was painted by Charles Fairfax Murray "who did all the rest of the pictures, with the exception of the one on page 1, which was by Burne-Jones," and George Wardle did some of the ornamental pattern work as well as "all the coloured letters." Morris's collaboration with these men is important to realize because from the outset he "had not intended to do all the work by himself, allocating various parts of it to his friends and fellow-workers, as had been done among medieval craftsmen."[13] Cooperative design, in other words, dominates the book from execution to finished product.

Like *The Defence of Guenevere* volume, the poems in *A Book of Verse* exhibit extreme self-reflection, as the title itself suggests. For this is not simply "a book of verse," it is something far more particular and concrete—*A Book of Verse* in which those four words, which are separable terms in a purely linguistic grammar, have been imaginatively transformed into a kind of proper noun. This effect is achieved partly through the allusion to the specific phrase in Fitzgerald's poem, and partly through the decision to make the book a unique object.

This kind of self-reflexiveness in the title appears throughout the book. In "Rest from Seeking," for example, a "heart that cravest love" is summoned by the textual voice to "come at last to me" (see fig. 17). The poem distinctly recalls various religious poems, especially those of Christina Rossetti (for example "Rest," published in 1862 in *Goblin Market and Other Poems*). But Morris's poem is entirely secular, and it invokes the image of a heavenly rest only to localize it in a purely textual immediacy:

> Draw nigh, draw nigh beloved! think of these
> Who stand about, as well-wrought images,
> Earless and eyeless as the whispering trees.   (13–15)

To this point the poem has supplied no linguistic referents for the pronoun "these." The only figures we have seen to "stand about" this poem are its decorative and calligraphic figurations, here cited—at the linguistic level—as "images." But the word carries a double burden in a highly decorative text like this one, for if it calls our attention to the poem as an artistic and bibliographical composition, it seeks as well a specifically semantic reference in the poem. The wit of this passage is to summon those images to make their semantic

REST FROM SEEKING.

O WEARY seeker over land and sea
O heart that cravest love perpetually,
Nor knowst his name, come now at last to me!

Come, thirst of love thy lips too long have borne
Hunger of love thy heart hath long outworn;
Speech hadst thou but to call thyself forlorn.

The seeker finds now, the parched lips are led
To sweet full streams, the hungry heart is fed
And song springs up from moans of sorrow dead.

Draw nigh, draw nigh, and tell me of thy tale
In words grown sweet since all the woe did fail
Show me wherewith thou didst thy woe bewail.

Draw nigh, draw nigh beloved! think of these
Who stand about, as well-wrought images,
Earless and eyeless as the whispering trees.

I think the sky calls living none but three,
The God that looketh thence, and thee and me;
And He made us, but we made Love to be.

17. William Morris, "Rest from Seeking," from decorated manuscript *A Book of Verse* (1870).

appearance in the work. This they do literally, as the formal simile in line 14 explicitly tells us. In the context, this simile is transformed into a kind of concrete thing—literally, the "image" of a poetical figure.

Having been summoned, the figures unfold their further linguistic presences:

> I think the sky calls living none but three
> The God that looketh thence, and thee and me;
> And he made us, but we made Love to be.
>
> Think not of Time then; for thou shalt not die
> How soon soever shall the World go by,
> And nought be left but God and thou and I.

What sky is this, we might ask. William Carlos Williams would later show us how to pose and answer such a question:

> Your thighs are appletrees
> whose blossoms touch the sky.
> Which sky? The sky
> where Watteau hung a lady's
> slipper.
>
> ("Portrait of a Lady," 1–5)

It is the sky of imagination, and all the beings in that sky, including the sky itself, are the creations of art. Most immediately, the sky is the heaven of the poem that has been executed on pages 13 to 14 of *A Book of Verse*. It is the voice of Beauty, revealed here as the God of Love, to which we now attend; and as that voice summons its listener, the latter enters the poem and is transformed into one of the text's wordmakers:

> Draw nigh, draw nigh, and tell me of thy tale
> In words grown sweet since all the woe did fail
> Show me wherewith thou didst thy woe bewail.

The "living . . . three" in the poem are not the traditional Trinity, they are rather textual positions in a poetical economy: signifier, signified, referent. "Thee and me" stand most immediately for the signifier and the signified, whereas the referent—"The God that looketh thence" from the text—is language conceived as a particular materialized formation. (I suppose it is needless to say that most of the features of a text like this are linguistically transformational, and so may be seen to occupy any of the three textual positions. The poem recalls, in this respect, a work like Blake's "The Lamb," which spins out a similar textual trinity in the figures of its child, lamb, and Jesus.)

All the poems in *A Book of Verse* come to us with elaborately decorated borders of leafage and flowers. This feature of the text is especially important for a work like "A Garden by the Sea" (see fig. 18).

> I know a little garden-close,
> Set thick with lily and red rose,
> Where I would wander if I might
> From dewy morn to dewy night
> And have one with me wandering.
>
> And though within it no birds sing,
> And though no pillared house is there
> And though the apple-boughs are bare
> Of fruit and blossom, would to God
> Her feet upon the green grass trod
> And I beheld them as before.   (1–11)

This garden appears throughout the book in the decorative borders, and in "A Garden by the Sea" the "garden-close" is specifically glimpsed in the border's trellis, which is twined with, among other flowers and leafage, a series of briar-roses. The allusion to Keats in line six is a textual emblem more than anything else, a sign that the garden is a place of imagination and erotic desire.

Indeed, the act of poetical surmise initiated in these two stanzas is the beginning of the fulfillment of that imaginative desire. The empty and absent garden appears as this literal text, which seems to be in the act of creating itself as its own garden of desire. The absent presences of the second stanza thus succeed to more positive figurations in the next stanza:

> There comes a murmur from the shore
> And in the close two fair streams are
> Drawn from the purple hills afar
> Drawn down unto the restless sea . . .
> Whose murmur comes unceasingly
> Unto the place for which I cry.   (12–15, 19–20)

A GARDEN BY THE SEA

I KNOW a little garden-close
Set thick with lily and red rose,
Where I would wander if I might
From dewy morn to dewy night
And have one with me wandering

And though within it no birds sing,
And though no pillared house is there,
And though the apple-boughs are bare
Of fruit and blossom, would to God
Her feet upon the green grass trod
And I beheld them as before.

There comes a murmur from the shore,
And in the close two fair streams are
Drawn from the purple hills afar
Drawn down unto the restless sea:
Dark hills whose heath-bloom feeds no bee,
Dark shore no ship has ever seen,
Tormented by the billows green
Whose murmur comes unceasingly
Unto the place for which I cry

For which I cry both day and night,

18. William Morris, "A Garden by the Sea," from decorated manuscript *A Book of Verse* (1870).

At this point the next stanza begins at the foot of page 31 with the line "For which I cry both day and night." The garden with its hills and shore, its sea and pair of streams, remains a linguistic desire barely glimpsed in the decorative borders—something longed for but not in fact seen.

The importance of *A Book of Verse*'s physical composition now becomes dramatically apparent. As the reader turns from page 31 to page 32 (see fig. 19) the "little garden-close" suddenly acquires a new level of substantiality in the "little" picture set at the "close" of the poem. All the linguistically surmised features of the place are there, and in the center walks the poet's beloved, whose "feet upon the green grass trod." She is, appropriately, reading "a book of verse," awaiting the arrival of her lover.

Significantly, the scene in the picture does not appear as "Dark" and "Tormented," as it did in stanza three:

> Dark hills whose heath-bloom feeds no bee,
> Dark shore no ship has ever seen,
> Tormented by the billows green   (16–18)

The scene in the miniature—by contrast, and like the work's bright border decorations—appears rich and unshadowed. Nevertheless, the picture's strongly defined frame emphasizes its separation from the poem's language of desire. The world of the garden, which is closer at the poem's end, remains unentered by the speaker:

> Yet tottering as I am and weak
> Still have I left a little breath
> To seek within the jaws of death
> An entrance to that happy place. . . .   (26–29)

Detailed study of *A Book of Verse* would show the many ways Morris integrates the book's bibliographical features to the texts of his verse. The calligraphy and the decorated capitals demand, it seems to me, a special study in themselves. The use of borders is also striking. All the poems are set in frames on each of the pages, but in some the right margin is filled with the leaf, flower, or trelliswork we saw in "A Garden by the Sea." In such cases the lines of the verse stand far from the frame and the margin, and embed themselves in the foliage.

Other poems, however, like "The Weariness of November" and "Love Alone," have a minimum of decorative work at the right margin, and the lines are allowed to run to the frame, and sometimes

A GARDEN BY THE SEA

For which I let slip all delight,
Whereby I grow both deaf and blind,
Careless to win, unskilled to find,
And quick to lose what all men seek.

Yet tottering as I am and weak
Still have I left a little breath
To seek within the jaws of death
An entrance to that happy place,
To seek the unforgotten face
Once seen once kissed, once reft from me
Anigh the murmuring of the sea

19. William Morris, "A Garden by the Sea," from decorated manuscript *A Book of Verse* (1870).

beyond the frame. In "The Weariness of November" the poem's frame functions brilliantly in relation to the lineation design (see fig. 20). The striking question put at the end of the first stanza visualizes itself bibliographically:

> Art thou so weary that no world there seems
> Beyond these four walls, hung with pain and dreams?
>
> (6–7)

One must actually see the page to appreciate how Morris has translated the frame of this text into an iconograph of the "four walls" named in these lines; and to appreciate as well how a freedom from "pain and dreams" is figured in the way the lines make random breaches in the wall to the right. The poem's frame is what the text itself calls a "Strange image of the dread eternity" (19) that closes off desire from what the text names "the real world" (8). That enclosure, however, like the loss of hope and the defeats of love celebrated throughout the book, becomes the occasion of freedom and deliverance. As the final pair of lines (20–21) both show and tell,

> In [such] void patience how can these have part,
> These outstretched feverish hands, this restless heart?

The answer is, as this handmade poem illustrates, that it can and cannot. Framed and closed in, "cabinned, cribbed, confined," the feverish hands repeatedly—and even ultimately—find a calligraphic escape from the four walls hung with the pain and dreams of the text's restless heart.[14]

If one turned at this point to Morris's Kelmscott Press edition of *Poems by the Way*, where several works from *A Book of Verse* also appear, the physical differences between the individual texts and the books as a whole would strike one immediately. One does not have to elaborate meanings here, the differences are, as Morris might have said, "a thing to mind." We have moved from an illuminated manuscript to a printed text partly designed as an act of homage to the fifteenth century. The texts from *A Book of Verse* are completely reconstituted, not so much at the linguistic level—though differences appear there—as in the physical presentation of the poems. *A Book of Verse* is designed page by page, as we saw so dramatically in "A Gar-

THE WEARINESS OF NOVEMBER.

I.

Are thine eyes weary? is thy heart too sick
To struggle any more with doubt, and thought
Whose formless veil draws darkening now and thick
Across thee e'en as smoke-tinged mist-wreaths, brought
Down a fair dale, to make it blind and nought?
Art thou so weary that no world there seems
Beyond these four walls, hung with pain and dreams?

II.

Look out upon the real world, where the moon,
Half-way twixt root and crown of these high trees,
Turns the dead midnight into dreamy noon,
Silent and full of wonders; for the breeze
Died at the sunset, and no images,
No hopes of day are left in sky or earth —
Is it not fair, and of most wondrous worth?

III.

Yea I have looked, and seen November there;
The changeless seal of change it seemed to be,
Fair death of things, that living once, were fair;
Bright sign of loneliness too great for me;
Strange image of the dread eternity;
In whose void patience how can these have part,
These outstretched feverish hands, this restless heart?

20. William Morris, "The Weariness of November," from decorated manuscript *A Book of Verse* (1870).

den by the Sea." It is very Blakean in this respect. *Poems by the Way*, on the contrary, is designed opening by opening, Morris's famous late imagination of how a properly designed book should be conceived and executed. In such circumstances "A Garden by the Sea," for example, appears a very different work (see fig. 21). The page opening where it begins ties it closely to the preceding poem, "On the Edge of the Wilderness," which concludes on the verso opposite. The red-inked refrain lines of the latter make a particularly strong contrast with the black-inked "A Garden by the Sea," and especially with the large decorated capital that dominates the poem's first page and forces the initial stanza into its unusual printed format.

In *Poems by the Way* Morris wants us to read this typographically rendered poetry as much with our eyes as with our minds. This is what he had done with the illuminated manuscript *A Book of Verse*, but while he was seeking for a similar effect in his earlier printed works, his desires went largely unrealized. As we have seen, the desires are traceable chiefly at the linguistic level of a book like *The Defence of Guenevere and Other Poems*. How differently those poems appear when Morris republishes them in his splendid 1892 Kelmscott Press edition! All the texts issued at Kelmscott Press put us on the brink of a new world of poetry. They are the forebears not merely of early modernist procedures like imagism, vorticism, and objectivism, but of important later developments in visual and concrete poetry.

All that is a story in itself, though it has yet to be properly told. I close this preliminary chapter of the tale with a glance at the last two books which Morris printed before he embarked on his Kelmscott Press adventure. These were *The House of the Wolfings* (1889) and *The Roots of the Mountains* (1890). Both were published by Reeves and Turner, but the key historical fact to know is that Morris went back, after a twenty-year hiatus, to Chiswick Press to have the books printed. Morris, with the help of his friend Emery Walker, designed the book himself, and chose the paper, ink, and typeface. The font used for the text is in each case Basel Roman, though the earlier book chooses an "e" with a slanted bar where the later book has a horizontal bar.

The title pages of each of these books are eloquent revelations of how materialized Morris's imagination had finally become. Both print the title in Caslon capitals below which, in Basel capitals, appears a set of verses. In each case the text is executed primarily as

And can I die now that thou biddest live?   On the Edge
What joy this space 'twixt birth and death can of the Wil-
give.   derness.
Can we depart, who are so happy here?

A GARDEN BY THE SEA.

A Garden by
the Sea.

 KNOW a little
garden-close,
Set thick with lily and
red rose,
Where I would wan-
der if I might
From dewy morn to
dewy night,
And have one with me
wandering.

And though within it no birds sing,
And though no pillared house is there,
And though the apple-boughs are bare
Of fruit and blossom, would to God
Her feet upon the green grass trod,
And I beheld them as before.

There comes a murmur from the shore,
And in the close two fair streams are,
Drawn from the purple hills afar,
Drawn down unto the restless sea:
Dark hills whose heath-bloom feeds no bee,

21. William Morris, "A Garden by the Sea," from *Poems by the Way*
(Kelmscott edition, 1891).

a design of words and lettering. The story of the title page of *The House of the Wolfings* tells it all (see fig. 22). According to H. Buxton Forman, who was at the Chiswick Press when the *Wolfings'* title page was being set, the wording of the title was altered simply because Morris did not like the typographical appearance of the title's fourth and fifth lines. An extra word was added to improve the text's physique.

Even more startling, however, is the way Morris treated the set of verses on the title page. They were, in the words of Henry Halliday Sparling, "written to measure."[15] By this Sparling means they were composed to fit not a metrical measure but the physical space on the title page. As Morris reportedly said to Forman, who had protested changing the title of the work merely to gain a visual felicity:

> Now what would you say if I told you that the verses on the title-page were written just to fill up the great white lower half? Well, that was what happened![16]

Forman did not record his response to this revelation. Yet it is clear that Morris's verses here are no less strong for having been written to a rule imposed by the mind of the eye, rather than the eye of the mind.

The title page of *The House of the Wolfings* was a forecast of what he would do on a massive scale with his Kelmscott Press books. The example of *The Earthly Paradise* is particularly striking. Recollect that Morris's first attempt at a complete marriage of bibliographical and linguistic elements was made in the late 1860s with the poem he was writing then, *The Earthly Paradise*. The 1860's project ended in failure, but it was resurrected in the 1890s as the culminant work of Morris's life.

The Kelmscott Press *Earthly Paradise* appeared between May 1896 and June 1897, in eight volumes. After its first three volumes were published (May–August 1896) Morris died, so that he did not live to see the actual completion of his great work. Nevertheless, all eight volumes had been in production for some time, so that Morris was kept only from executing final proof corrections to the (now long-established) text.

We have only to consider the work's initial ornamented opening, with the title page of the prologue and its prose argument on the verso (refer to fig. 4) and (on the recto) the first thirteen lines of the prologue's text (see fig. 23). The two pages obviously mirror each

A TALE OF THE HOUSE OF THE WOLFINGS AND ALL THE KIND-REDS OF THE MARK WRITTEN IN PROSE AND IN VERSE BY WILLIAM MORRIS.

WHILES IN THE EARLY WINTER EVE
WE PASS AMID THE GATHERING NIGHT
SOME HOMESTEAD THAT WE HAD TO LEAVE
YEARS PAST ; AND SEE ITS CANDLES BRIGHT
SHINE IN THE ROOM BESIDE THE DOOR
WHERE WE WERE MERRY YEARS AGONE
BUT NOW MUST NEVER ENTER MORE,
AS STILL THE DARK ROAD DRIVES US ON.
E'EN SO THE WORLD OF MEN MAY TURN
AT EVEN OF SOME HURRIED DAY
AND SEE THE ANCIENT GLIMMER BURN
ACROSS THE WASTE THAT HATH NO WAY ;
THEN WITH THAT FAINT LIGHT IN ITS EYES
A WHILE I BID IT LINGER NEAR
AND NURSE IN WAVERING MEMORIES
THE BITTER-SWEET OF DAYS THAT WERE.

LONDON 1889 : REEVES AND TURNER 196 STRAND.

22. William Morris, *A Tale of the House of the Wolfings*, title page (1889).

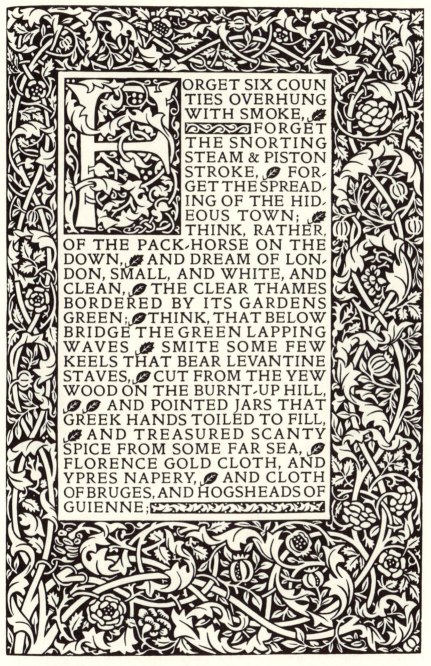

FORGET SIX COUNTIES OVERHUNG WITH SMOKE, FORGET THE SNORTING STEAM & PISTON STROKE, FORGET THE SPREADING OF THE HIDEOUS TOWN; THINK, RATHER, OF THE PACK-HORSE ON THE DOWN, AND DREAM OF LONDON, SMALL, AND WHITE, AND CLEAN, THE CLEAR THAMES BORDERED BY ITS GARDENS GREEN; THINK, THAT BELOW BRIDGE THE GREEN LAPPING WAVES SMITE SOME FEW KEELS THAT BEAR LEVANTINE STAVES, CUT FROM THE YEW WOOD ON THE BURNT-UP HILL, AND POINTED JARS THAT GREEK HANDS TOILED TO FILL, AND TREASURED SCANTY SPICE FROM SOME FAR SEA, FLORENCE GOLD CLOTH, AND YPRES NAPERY, AND CLOTH OF BRUGES, AND HOGSHEADS OF GUIENNE;

23. William Morris, *The Earthly Paradise*, "Prologue. The Wanderers" lines 1–13 (Kelmscott edition, 1896).

other, and the opening as a whole presents an image of extreme textual ornamentation. Borders between decorative materials and linguistic text are established only to be overrun everywhere. One observes in particular the ornamental work surrounding the boxed title and author-line on the verso and the heavily decorated capital on the recto. In each case the leafwork defined at the margins has moved into bibliographical spaces normally occupied by typeface alone.

Equally important for creating the extraordinary (even excessive) richness of these pages is the choice of typeface and line layout. The decision to print everything in capitals recalls the manner of certain medieval manuscripts. In a culture that largely imagines print as a vehicle for linguistic meaning, the effect is to foreground textuality as such, turning words from means to ends-in-themselves. The text here is hard to read, is too thick with its own materialities. It resists any processing that would simply treat it as a set of referential signs pointing beyond themselves to a semantic content. This text declares its radical self-identity.

The declaration is especially clear in the recto's text where a collision of contradictory signals holds our attention. The text, that is to say, comprises a sequence of rhyming couplets, but the lines run margin to margin, creating another "spatial rhyme" with the prose layout of the verso text. When Morris signals the couplet endings with small leaf ornaments, we "see" the couplet forms, see language as a poetical medium in which time gets measured out. But we see it through a sign that is dominantly spatial and iconic. A border or distinction is thereby both established and violated at once, much as we see the general border between verbal text and visual ornament violated at all points on these remarkable pages.

This kind of textual scene short-circuits referential reading procedures. Through the apparent temporalities of language we plunge into a different order of things.

❃ Why not say "transported to a different order of things?" These poems are *about* being transported, aren't they? And isn't that why they seem so odd—perhaps even so uninteresting—to a modernist imagination?

I can't answer for your "modernist imagination." I only say that, yes, these poems *are* about being transported. But their importance lies in the stylistic moves they take to accomplish their ends. Like

Poe's and Baudelaire's work, Morris's affects not inspiration and spontaneity so much as craft and extreme deliberateness. The textual move is the opposite of transcendental because we are not borne away with these pages, we are borne down by them. The work forces us to attend to its immediate and iconic condition, as if the words were images or objects in themselves, as if they were *values* in themselves (rather than vehicles for delivering some further value or meaning). Everything here is what it appears to be; meaning is complete and apparent. There is no fly to be gotten out of the fly bottle.

Morris's poetry in a Kelmscott Press format—recall the opening stanza of "A Garden by the Sea"—has crossed a boundary that marks off some distinctively twentieth-century poetic and semiotic innovations. Scholars of the book have often condemned Morris's typographical work because its extreme physicality interferes with the text's "readability." Even those sympathetic to the beauty of Morris's typographical work, like William Peterson, accede to this view.[17] But to anyone who is more interested in the poetical rather than the expository functions of texts, Morris's Kelmscott poetry will appear as remarkable in its way as those equally "unreadable" texts engraved one hundred years before by William Blake. And to anyone interested in the history of twentieth-century poetry, Morris's career will be seen for what in fact it was: a profound, a deeply influential, precursive event.

2

Composition as Explanation (of Modern and Postmodern Poetries)

In "Literature and the Living Voice" Yeats observed that "English literature, alone of great literatures because the newest of them all, has all but completely shaped itself in the printing press."[1] In truth the history of modernist writing could be written as a history of the modernist book. Were one to write that history, Ezra Pound would appear once again the crucial point of departure. Like the Alps for a western imagination, he and his *Cantos* prove—for better and for worse—unevadable:

> There they are, you will have to go a long way round
> if you want to avoid them.[2]

Bunting's famous lines go to the heart of the matter: that Pound's work has a substantial *thingness* to it, a kind of hard objective presence. The title of the poem—"On the Fly-Leaf of Pound's Cantos"—defines the modernist perspective that Yeats had called attention to.

Consider the three books that first printed Cantos I–XXX. Their significance is completely involved with the late nineteenth-century's Renaissance of Printing. To understand how deeply this is true we have to retreat in time to the earliest period of Pound's literary life—to the year, in fact, when he (later) said he "began the Cantos" (even though, as he also said, he "didn't get [them] onto paper" at that time").[3] In a letter to his mother from Hamilton College in 1904 Pound said he was writing an "Essay on early poetry of Wm Morris" (Carpenter, 48). Shortly afterwards, during the intensities of his affair with H. D., Pound's involvement with Morris and Pre-Raphaelitism had deepened considerably. Not only does his early poetry display the influence of several Pre-Raphaelite styles (Morris, Rossetti, and Swinburne especially), Pound shows himself fully aware of the late nineteenth-century's printing revolution that Pre-Raphaelitism had done so much to inaugurate and advance.

That awareness is materialized in the unique (handmade) volume he titled *Hilda's Book*, his first book of poetry.[4] Though a gift to H. D., the book is an act of homage to Pre-Raphaelitism and the ideal of the troubadour poet it passed on to him. *Hilda's Book* is a small volume of verse, mostly handwritten in an ornamental script, bound in vellum. As H. D. wrote later in *End to Torment*,

> He brought me the Portland, Maine, Thomas Mosher reprint of the Iseult and Tristram story. He called me Is-hilda and wrote a sonnet a day: he bound them in a parchment folder. (23)

Like Morris when he founded the Kelmscott Press, Thomas Mosher began his famous press (the same year as Kelmscott, 1891) in conscious imitation of the master printers of the fifteenth century. In the imagination of those swept up in the late nineteenth-century's Renaissance of Printing, the physical presentation of texts was a fundamental feature of their expressiveness. The material form in which one read "the Iseult and Tristram story" had to be thought as important as the story itself.

The point was not simply that writing ought to look handsome or attractive. More crucial were the historical meanings that could be carried by a book's "ornamental" features. Pound apparently learned the power of graphic and typographic book production from Morris and Pre-Raphaelitism. But as his move to London shows, he understood that Morris's Kelmscott adventure was not the only model available to someone interested in expressive book design. In fact, two great bibliographical styles emerged in English book production of the 1890s.

The most celebrated of the two is the Kelmscott style. As we have seen, Morris's books were consciously designed to recall the revolutionary bookwork of the fifteenth century—and especially those early printed books that stood closest to richly decorated medieval manuscript books scripted in closely written Gothic bookhands. For the modern eye, however, such a style can create reading problems. In Kelmscott Press books a recollective visual design is so paramount that legibility becomes almost a second-order goal of the printing work.

The rich weight of Morris's Kelmscott texts would ultimately stand as only one pole of the imagination that drove the late nineteenth-century Renaissance of Printing. The other was represented by the textual clarities made famous in the work of the Bodley Head Press. For Ezra Pound, Bodley Head proved as formative a resource as Kelmscott.

Begun jointly by Elkin Mathews and John Lane in 1889, Bodley Head chiefly published serious and experimental writing in handsome book designs at relatively cheap prices. Printing runs were small as the books were being offered to a special audience. Indeed, the press succeeded in no small part because it helped to consolidate such an audience. To be a Bodley Head author, or reader, defined you as a certain type of person—aesthetic and very modern.

Bodley Head's most famous publication was probably *The Yellow Book*, but the firm's authors, book designers, and illustrators included the most prominent figures of the period. Unlike Morris's Kelmscott books, the Bodley Head book featured a clear and readable page, where beauty emerged as a function of the elegance and simplicity of arrangement. The approach to book design, which shows the influence of Whistler, was executed by men like Charles Ricketts, Charles Jacobi, and especially Walter Blaikie. Ricketts founded the famous Vale Press with Charles Shannon; Jacobi was general manager of the legendary Chiswick Press, and Blaikie (of T. and A. Constable) was, next to Morris, probably the most respected and influential "artist printer" of the period.

In 1894 the partnership between Mathews and Lane was dissolved and each went his own way. Mathews retained some of the most prominent of the old Bodley Head authors, including Wilde, Lionel Johnson, and Yeats. Of the two original partners, Mathews was distinctly the less aggressive entrepreneur. His relatively noncommercial approach to publishing, so unlike Lane's, was part of the overall scrupulousness that appealed to the authors he printed.

This history is important to recall because when Pound went to London in 1908 he immediately sought out Mathews as a possible publisher for his work. The two hit it off immediately and Mathews became Pound's principal publisher. The poet's first four books issued by Mathews—between 1909 and 1916—were in fact all printed at Chiswick Press. Jacobi had been manager of this old and distinguished firm. As we have already seen, at the outset of his career Morris sought out Chiswick Press to print his books. He returned to Chiswick again, in the late 1880s, when he and Emery Walker began the bookmaking collaboration that would result in the founding of Kelmscott Press.

So far as Pound's work is concerned, two matters are especially important here. First, Pound from the start conceived his own work in the context of the late nineteenth-century Renaissance of Printing. He understood what had been happening in that movement and he sympathized with its goals. Second, he kept close contact with the actual design and production of his own work. He published his first printed book *A Lume Spento* himself and afterwards he never abandoned a practical involvement in all the productive aspects of his writing. By the time he came to publish the first book installments of the *Cantos*, Pound was knowledgeable and experienced in the making of books.

The first two volumes were *A Draft of XVI. Cantos* (1925) and *A Draft of the Cantos 17–27* (1928). The former was printed and published in Paris at William Bird's Three Mountains Press in a large format (39.2 × 26.2 cm.). The initials and headpieces were designed by Henry Strater under Pound's careful instructions. The second book (39.1 × 25.9 cm.) was meant to be uniform with the first. It was published in London by John Rodker and printed in England by J. Curwen and Sons, Ltd. The initials and headpieces were executed by Gladys Hynes. The colophons for both books clearly indicate their lavish and expensive production values. The third volume was *A Draft of XXX Cantos* (1930), published in Paris by Nancy Cunard's Hours Press. The format was much smaller (21.2 × 14.8 cm.), the headpieces and colored printing were absent, and the initials were designed in a vorticist style by Pound's wife Dorothy. All three books are printed in the same modernized Caslon typeface, although the smaller format of the 1930 volume necessitated the choice of a smaller font.[5]

The most striking visual feature of the 1925 and 1928 volumes is their eclecticism. Although the style of the titles of the different *Cantos* varies, all the titles recall medieval calligraphy or decorative printing. Indeed, Pound's titles distinctly recall the uncial calligraphic forms that stand behind subsequent medieval developments in lettering. The same kind of antique allusion appears in the ornamented (or even historiated) initials, as well as in the headpieces (recalling the woodcuts of early printed books). The red and black printing functions in a similar way. In these textual features we see the strong influence of the Kelmscott book, which is distinguished by elaborate ornamental materials, including decorative capitals and two-color printing in red and black.[6] The typeface, on the other hand, so clearly modern, makes a sharp contrast with the medieval-ism of the books' other features. As in Yeats's Dun Emer/Cuala Press books, one sees here a compromise, or marriage, of the different styles of Morris on the one hand and Blaikie on the other—of Kelmscott and Bodley Head.

This bibliographical contrast also helps to define the historical meaning, or argument, which these two installments of the *Cantos* are making. Canto I launches the *Cantos* project in explicitly biblio-graphical terms: the voyage of Odysseus is a matter of linguistic translation and book production. From Pound's vantage, then, it would be important to express that historical subject at every level of the work. The stylistic contrast between his books' ornament and typography map the history he is interested in. The pages of these books recollect at the design level the epochal (bibliographical) events of the fifteenth century and the late nineteenth century. The *Cantos* project locates itself within that historical nexus.

A Draft of XXX Cantos is uniform with the two previous books in that Pound continues to exploit a contrast between the ornamental initials and the body of the text. In this case, however, the contrast operates wholly within a relatively "modern" horizon. The typeface is modernized Caslon, but because the initials are so agressively vor-ticist, the typeface functions now as the sign of an earlier historical or stylistic moment. From a purely personal point of view the initials recollect Pound's London years, and the beginning of his "modern-ism" (in the most restricted sense of the term). At the level of the work's bibliographical symbology, *A Draft of XXX Cantos* has moved a step away from the Pre-Raphaelite and aesthetic position recol-lected in the first two volumes.

The physical presentation of these three books thus constitutes a display of their meanings. Book design here defines not merely the immediate historical horizon of Pound's *Cantos* project, it declares the meaningfulness of historical horizons as such. In doing this, the work equally declares its commitment to a fully materialized un-derstanding of language. The *Cantos* summons up the power and authority of the most elementary forms of language, its systems of signifiers, and it apprehends these signifiers as historical artifacts. The graphic presentation of Pound's books is thus made an index of their aims. Through book design Pound makes an issue of language's physique, deliberateness, and historicality.

꙰

The history inscribed in Pound's initial project for the *Cantos* has been preserved in other important records of the period. Many of the most influential works of the Harlem Renaissance—for instance Hughes's *The Weary Blues* (1926), various books by Countee Cullen, Alain Locke's anthology *The New Negro* (1925)—all display the profound effect produced by the graphic and bibliographic revolution at the end of the nineteenth century. In these cases the style has taken a definitively modernist step beyond medievalism and aestheticism; nonetheless, that step would not have been possible without the historical inertia generated out of the late Victorians. Nor did their influence extend only to experimentalist writing. Hardy's first book of verse, *Wessex Poems* (1898), marries the new aesthetic style of text presentation with a series of sketches (by Hardy himself) "illustrating" the symbolic topography being constructed by the book.

The Yeatsian record—so crucial in every way—tells a similar story. When Yeats tried to summarize modern poetry in his *Oxford Book of Modern Verse* (1936) he made a famous gesture to modernism's aesthetic and Pre-Raphaelite inheritance. He printed as the first text in his collection a notable passage from Pater's *The Renaissance*. An unusual choice of text, but most startling of all was its graphic appearance: Yeats reformatted Pater's lush prose as a free verse poem (see fig. 24). Readers have generally taken free form as an emblem of modernism's experimental advance beyond its nineteenth-century precursors. But the truth is that those free verse forms emerged in part because Morris and some of his contemporaries had begun to work consciously with the spatial features of the page and the book as they might be resources for poetic effects.

❋ Mallarmé's experiments with the spatial form of the page are surely more to the point, don't you think?

That's been the view of our traditional literary histories. But it's a narrow view, despite its apparent internationalism. We aren't discounting modernism's French connections by calling attention to others that were equally, and perhaps even more, significant. Kelmscott Press and Bodley Head locate historical relations that have been largely forgotten.

WALTER PATER

1839–1894

I   *Mona Lisa*

S HE is older than the rocks among which she sits;
  Like the Vampire,
She has been dead many times,
And learned the secrets of the grave;
And has been a diver in deep seas,
And keeps their fallen day about her;
And trafficked for strange webs with Eastern merchants;
And, as Leda,
Was the mother of Helen of Troy,
And, as St Anne,
Was the mother of Mary;
And all this has been to her but as the sound of lyres and
      flutes,
And lives
Only in the delicacy
With which it has moulded the changing lineaments,
And tinged the eyelids and the hands.

24. Walter Pater, "Mona Lisa," from Yeats's *Oxford Book of Modern Verse 1892–1935* (1936).

In any event, at stake here is something more important than establishing clear lines of historical causation. Only certain aspects of English Pre-Raphaelitism and French symbolism seemed important to the programs of modernism. The format of Yeats's text from Pater is a bibliographically coded message drawing a historical relation between Pre-Raphaelitism, aestheticism, and modernism. The semantic content of the message is carried by the graphic features. This ascension of the signifier speaks on one hand about the coming of modernism, and constructs on the other Yeats's version of its prehistory. The text is an emblem for a poetry that means to come to its senses.

Yeats tells an odd history here and he tells it in an odd way. What is even more odd, I suspect that he took his immediate inspiration for rewriting Pater's work from Louis Zukofsky. The last section of *An "Objectivists" Anthology* (1932), headed "Collaborations," prints a series of texts that have been similarly "rewritten." Zukofsky apparently meant these "collaborations" to illustrate a distinction he wanted to draw between "sincerity" and "objectification" in poetry.[7] However immediate the relation between Yeats's Pater text and Zukofsky's anthology, both works illustrate the renewed interest that modern poets were taking in the materialities of poetic textualization.

So far I have been emphasizing the analogy between "composition" as it concerns the typographer and "composition" as it concerns the visual artist. Another analogy is possible, however, and has been equally important. "Composition" is an activity of musicians, and the printed page may equally be produced as a kind of musical score, or set of directions for the audition of verse and voice.

So far as modernism is concerned, Zukofsky is a key figure for such a project. As much as Pater he saw poetry as an aspiration—in both senses—toward the condition of music. His interest in the visual field of the page was finally auditional: the formatting of a text as a means for scoring the musical resources of poetry, including voice.

> Typography—certainly—if print and the arrangement of it will help to tell how the voice should sound.

Zukofsky is aware that modernism, and in particular the work of Pound, offered another very different way of thinking about typography. His next sentence alludes to this other way, but sets it aside:

It is questionable on the other hand whether the letters of the alphabet can be felt as the Chinese feel their written characters. (*Anthology*, 20)

The (free verse) line from Zukofsky to the projectivist work of the 1950s is quite direct. It is a line for composing, in the musical sense, sound and speech patterns. If we look backwards from Zukofsky, this line—as we all know—is spun out of Whitman.

I recall these matters to contrast them with a very different tradition of the free verse movement. Morris did not write free verse, but his interest in the physique of poetry had its greatest impact on this other tradition, where "Writing as Composition" connects to the visual imagination of the painter, the graphic artist, and the typographer. (The poems on the title pages of both *The Roots of the Mountains* and *The House of the Wolfings* illustrate types of what we would now call "concrete poetry.") In the European context the tradition begins with Mallarmé and then explodes in Apollinaire's calligrammatology and Cendrars's stunning experiments in "Simultaneity." As I have already suggested, this alternative line—so far as American poetry is concerned—should be connected with the textual innovations of Emily Dickinson.[8] To see her verse as a kind of graffiti seems to me useful.

Pound's typographical experiments, glanced at by Zukofsky, have come to epitomize this other tradition for English readers. The visual tradition's most important modernist practitioner and theorist, however, was Robert Carlton ("Bob") Brown—that strange and arresting American, now academically forgotten, whose work culminates the extraordinary tradition of modern experimentalist writing.[9] The year that Nancy Cunard's Hours Press brought out Pound's *A Draft of XXX Cantos* (1930) also saw the appearance of Brown's polemical treatise on poetry and printing, *The Readies*. Each book is a conscious reimagination of the possibilities of poetic expression, and both situate themselves in the bibliographical renaissance that Morris had brought to a flash point.

The two works display very different emphases. *A Draft of XXX Cantos* looks directly back to the craft traditions revivified by the work of Morris. The book is handprinted on rag paper in the modern Caslon used by William Bird for his previous editions of Pound's Pre-Raphaelite cantos—a variant of the same font that had been resurrected by Chiswick Press in the nineteenth century, and that so captured the imagination of Morris.[10] Brown's work, by contrast, is a small pamphlet printed by machine on cheap chemical paper.

The difference Brown's book makes with Pound's is, however, conscious and deliberate. *The Readies* issues a hail and farewell to earlier dreamers of a revolutionary word.[11] Brown made his point even more dramatically a year earlier when he published his collection of (what shall we call them?) "optical poems" in the book *1450– 1950*, with its graphic dedication page (see fig. 25).[12] "Writing has been bottled up in books since the start," Brown playfully laments in *The Readies*; "It is time to pull out the stopper" (28).

Brown had been working at that stuck stopper since 1914, when he first read Stein's *Tender Buttons*, which seems to have completely transformed his sense of writing. "I began to see that a story might be anything . . . [and] didn't have to be a tangible hunk of bread interest. . . . Thank God for Gert Stein."[13] He "began to experiment for the first time," and when he struck off his optical poem "Eyes on the Half-Shell," Marcel Duchamp printed it in his journal *Blindman* in 1917 (see fig. 26). Brown later included it in his collection *1450– 1950*. His commentary on the text is important:

> I have since taken this for a symbol of what I have been trying to do in writing, off and on for fifteen years. . . . I like to look at it, merely sit and look at it, take it all in without moving an eye. It gives me more than rhymed poetry. It rhymes in my eyes. Here are Black Riders for me at last galloping across a blank page.[14]

Brown's optical poems can be misleading, can make one think that he is simply reconnecting with those innovative visual texts produced by Edward Lear, Lewis Carroll, and (before them) William Blake. Of course Brown's relation to these poets is important, but in his mind the optical poem does not at all require figural decorative ornaments. The physical medium of any kind of textuality—in a typographical mode the basic elements are paper, ink, cuts, and various type fonts—can be manipulated to the same effect.

> I'm for new methods of reading and writing and I believe the up-to-date reader deserves an eye-ful when he buys something to read. (*Readies*, 1)

Brown's idea was to immerse the reader in the print medium, much as the viewer is immersed in images at the cinema. "The Readies" is

1450

DEDICATED TO.

ALL MONKS WHO ILLUMINATED
MANUSCRIPTS — ALL EARLY
ORIENTAL ARTISTS — OMAR-
GUTENBERG - CAXTON--
JIMMY-THE-INK — BOCCACCIO -
RABELAIS — SHAKESPEARE-
DEFOE — GOYA — BLAKE-
STERNE - WHITMAN — CRANE-
STEIN — JOYCE — PAGLIACCI -
AND
MYSELF
1950

25. Robert Carlton Brown, *1450–1950*, dedication page (1929).

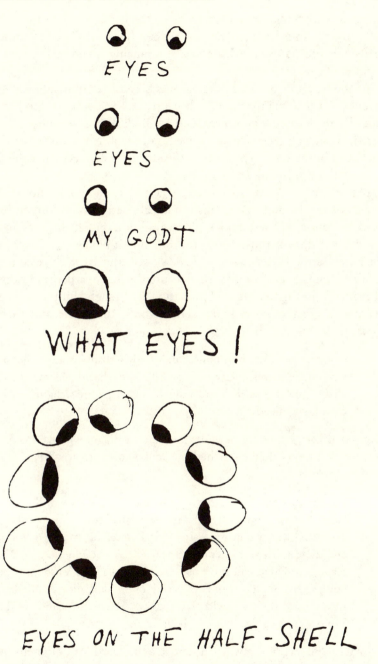

26. Robert Carlton Brown, "Eyes on the Half-Shell," from *1450–1950* (1929).

Brown's witty bibliographical takeoff on those recent modernist inventions, the "movies" and "talkies." When Brown declared "I bathe in Apollinaire" (*Readies*, 1), he was announcing his ideal linguistic experience.

At the center of Brown's program was his half-serious half-playful invention, a "reading machine." This apparatus was supposed to provide the reader with the power to read in all directions and at any speed, to change type size and type-face at will, to leap forward or backward in the text: to browse, to speedread, to connect any and all parts of the text in any and all ways.

Brown wants to overgo the recent advances of those who used fine-book production as a means to radical poetic innovation. So he puns his refusal of the bibliographical tradition on which Yeats and Pound had drawn, those "beautiful but dumb books as clumsy in their way as the Rozetti stone" (*Readies*, 40). But Brown's rejection is full of homage and admiration because the great earlier traditions of printing and manuscript illumination had taught him a "loving wonder, a great want-to-know about words, their here and their there, their this and their that":

> The monks in the beginning didn't do it so badly in their illuminated manuscripts, they retained a little of the healthy hieroglyphic, all Oriental books in ideogrammatic character are delights, early colophons splendid. (*Readies*, 39)

Even as Brown explicitly pays his respects to Blake, Morris, Pound and the traditions they cherished, he makes his turn toward a new world of words.

> For the first time in the history of mental optics there will exist a visual Literary Language sharply separated from the Speaking Tongue. Literary Language is Optical, speaking language Vocal, and the gap between them must spread till it becomes a gulf. My reading machine will serve as a wedge. Makers of words will be born; fresh, vital eye-words will wink out of dull, dismal, drooling type at startled smug readers here below. . . . The Revolution of the Word will be all over but the shouting. . . . (*Readies*, 39)

Brown's *jouissance* of the word anticipates the Derridean moment by forty years, and prophecies as well the practical emergence of computerized word-processing and hypertextual fields.

Blake, Rossetti, and Morris were inspirations rather than models. The point is made clearly in one of the texts printed in Brown's optical collection *1450–1950* (see e.g. fig. 27). The poles of 1450/1950 are defined by "ILLUMINATED MSS." on one hand and "ILLUMINATING / MOVIE SCRIPTS" on the other. Brown faces "forward," but with many glances "back" and sideways full of interest and respect. He keeps his eyes open in all directions. Most immediately, he looks to find on the contemporary scene those "makers of words" called for by *The Readies*.

The makers were alive and very active. Brown's manifesto was followed almost immediately by his anthology *Readies for Bob Brown's Machine* (1931), an extraordinary collection of liberated texts supplied to Brown by some of the most innovative writers of his age: Williams, McAlmon, Harry Crosby, Stein, Sidney Hunt, Pound, Hemingway, and many others. When the afterhistory of modernism is written, this collection—along with its better known counterpart published a year later, Zukofsky's *An "Objectivists" Anthology*—will be recognized as a work of signal importance.

Readies for Bob Brown's Machine is a far more European work of modernism than Zukofsky's anthology. Unlike the latter, Brown's book displays a conscious appropriation of the many textual and bibliographical innovations that had been sweeping across Europe for twenty years and more. Futurism, dada, simultaneism, zaum, vorticism, cubism, German expressionism: all these movements have left their visible marks on Brown's collection, whereas in Zukofsky's gathering—except for imagism—the firestorm of modernism's experimental energies has been translated and modified. In each anthology the rules of a liberated verse are largely governed by intuitions of the eye, but in one case the eye is more interested in composing temporal forms, whereas spatiality dominates in the other. Besides, Brown's book—so far as poetry as such is concerned—enters wilder territory, as a casual glance at almost any page of the collection indicates. Sidney Hunt's "MORNINIGHT CAR (nocturnal day realm)," for example, distinctly recollects Brown's call in *The Readies* to "see words machinewise."

Black-Riders-Crash-by-hell-bent-for-leather-
uppercase-LOWERCASE-both————together-chanting-
valorously-Print-in-action-at——longlast-movable-
type-at-breakneck-gallop[. . .] daredevil-commaless-

I LIKE LOOKING BACK
AT THE
ILLUMINATED MSS. OF

1450
AND FORWARD
TO THE
MORE ILLUMINATING
MOVIE SCRIPTS OF
1950

I LIKE TO SEE
FLY SPECKS
ON YELLOWED PAGES
I LIKE TOO
LEAVING MY OWN ON
NEW ONES

MY FLY SPECK

27. Robert Carlton Brown, from *1450–1950* (1929).

Cossacks-astride-mustang-bronco————vocabularies-
leaning-farout-into-inky-night————   (37)

The word "uppercase" printed here in lowercase, the word "LOWER-
CASE" printed in uppercase: it is a small emblem of what Brown has
in his mind. Futurism supplies Brown with the trope of speed and
the wisdom of machines ("machinewise") that negotiates the field of
this particular text (see also fig. 28).

But speed is only one possible sign of the word revolution Brown
desires. Indeed, the trope emerges most immediately out of a very
different figure, the "Black-Riders" that set a pattern for the text's
"breakneck-gallop . . . into-inky-night." The phrase is an allusion to
Stephen Crane's first published book, *Black Riders and other lines*
(1895), which gave Brown "the only hint I have found of Moving
Reading," and which suggested to him "the dash of inky words at full
gallop across the plains of pure white pages" (*Readies*, 32–33).

It is worth pausing for a moment over Crane's book, which clearly
had a great influence on Brown. It was published (in New York) by
the recently established firm Copeland and Day, in conscious imitation of the bibliographical innovations championed by the Pre-Raphaelites and their inheritors.[15] The book comes with a Rossettian/
Bodley Head decorated cover (black with an embossed orchid design, and with the title and author's name stamped in gold). It was
printed in a run limited to five-hundred copies, with a few copies
issued in vellum. Most startling, however, at least if we think of
Brown's apparent obsession with futurist speed, is the extreme stillness of Crane's text page. The book consists of fifty-six short pieces,
each roman numbered and each set out on a page by itself, and
printed (in small capitals) high up on the page so as to leave a notable
space below the text.[16] The poems confront the reader as hieratic and
symbolist texts, and hardly as forerunners of futurism.

I

BLACK RIDERS CAME FROM THE SEA.
THERE WAS CLANG AND CLANG OF SPEAR AND
    SHIELD,
AND CLASH AND CLASH OF HOOF AND HEEL,
WILD SHOUTS AND THE WAVE OF HAIR
IN THE RUSH UPON THE WIND:
THUS THE RIDE OF SIN.

— 149 —

big .... stare ,,,,,,,,,,,,..............................
      E
     E Y E .. in womans back dis s o l v
      E
in shinyblackbarcktaxi swift u r n spurt suddn gon
t r a c kng ....van.sh.d....enema................
.... = ...
      . . = = . = . mouths = = =
=   = float= =   =   =
=   in   =   =   =   =   a =
= =   =   =   =   =
= =   =   glass =   =   =
=   =   =   universe   =   =   =
(angled)   (maze)   =   =   =   mouths
=   mad   =   red   =   =   =
c - o -a -l esce
         to a.   VIVVID   SHOUT
r e m b l e air ri-g-i d splintercrash glasssplinters-
hatter m e l t d e wy * . . . . .
infinothing
clearlip rigid s p h i n x e s r i g i d l ypass
r i g i d l y p a s s t h e r i g i d m o v i n g
s p h i n x e s m o v e l e s s m o v e r i g idly
r i g i d r i g i d-i-r-i-g-i-b-l-e s p h i n x e s n o
m o v e l e s s s p h i n x e s s p h i n c t e r --
c l utch spas m i call f l ash gone s p h i n x e s -
r i g i dirigible gone none
. . . SILK . . . STUN . . . SUN . . . STARE . .
rub glassrubbd clear for lst interlewd . . . ..
ringadoor of bellsuddn lizards swivelround . . . . .
jerka suddnstep bell of .ringabreath openrings oke
admits entering ting tang look cool smooth spread
divide conquer keen dawn celaknees (=) (=) furedge
cliff 2 solids:lk arrestfall torrents tenderbeach——
heaves v a l l eys MOUNDS v a l l eys MOUNDs
l o p e - d o w nup stingpringa lipskin s p h i n x e
spasspasm =ically l o v e dumb volubublimbs
liplip .nee.nee farNEARNEAReye temderintent-

28. Sidney Hunt, "MORNINIGHT CAR (nocturnal day realm)," from
Readies for Bob Brown's Machine (1931).

Though it might seem a relatively trivial matter, the decision to print the poems in small capitals pitched Crane's book into a novel imaginative direction, as Brown saw. The capitals, as well as the isolation of each poem on the page, draw one's attention to the poetry's material features, and ultimately to an awareness of poetry *as a system of material signifiers*. In *The Black Riders and other lines* what Brown saw were texts always collapsing in upon themselves:

> XLII
>
> I WALKED IN A DESERT.
>
> AND I CRIED,
>
> "AH, GOD, TAKE ME FROM THIS PLACE!"
>
> A VOICE SAID, "IT IS NO DESERT."
>
> I CRIED, "WELL, BUT—
>
> THE SAND, THE HEAT, THE VACANT HORIZON."
>
> A VOICE SAID, "IT IS NO DESERT."

> XLVI
>
> MANY RED DEVILS RAN FROM MY HEART
>
> AND OUT UPON THE PAGE,
>
> THEY WERE SO TINY
>
> THE PEN COULD MASH THEM.
>
> AND MANY STRUGGLED IN THE INK.
>
> IT WAS STRANGE
>
> TO WRITE IN THIS RED MUCK
>
> OF THINGS FROM MY HEART.

These are Barthesian writings, already fully conscious that the poetic field is self-signifying. The "I" walks in the white desert of the page, whose vacancy it populates by its walking, by the "lines" of Crane's title as they move out in a heroic but unfulfillable quest for completion.

In Crane's book the page appears under various forms—as snow, as desert, as psychic vacancy, and—most often—as itself, or part of itself:

> XLIV
>
> I WAS IN THE DARKNESS:
>
> I COULD NOT SEE MY WORDS
>
> NOR THE WISHES OF MY HEART.

THEN SUDDENLY THERE WAS GREAT LIGHT—

"LET ME INTO THE DARKNESS AGAIN."

The typographical wit of this text, where the "great light" comes as a small blank moment on the page, must have been a joy to Bob Brown's days. In another age and style that light was called (romantically) "inspiration" and "imagination."

The example of Crane, so important for Brown, helps to explain the latter's equal enthusiasm for Marinetti on one hand and for Pound on the other, for Sidney Hunt and for Gertrude Stein. Texts do not have to gallop to be free. "I have only to bend my finger in a beckon," Brown writes, "and words, birds of words, hop on it, chirping" (*Readies*, 4). Brown's own poetical texts may speed up or slow down, and they perform these operations in various ways.

We see this nowhere more clearly, perhaps, than in his splendid book *Words*, published by Hours Press in 1931. The book's subtitle, printed in microform type that requires either an eagle's eye or a magnifying glass to be read, tells its story simultaneously as a lexical and a typographical message: "I but bend my finger in a beckon and words, birds of words, hop on it, chirping." Brown runs a continuous gloss through his book in the form of such microform typescripts. The first page of "La Vie Americaine" provides an especially dramatic example of Brown's unusual semiotic imagination (see fig. 29). Carefully scrutinized, this page's microform gloss text delivers up its reading:

> I, who am God
> Wear lavender pyjamas and
> Pure poetry
> Should I, who am God
> Dirty my ear on the ground
> Striving to catch the
> Idiotic waltzing lilt of
> Rhyming red-eyed dervish
> Twirling white pink poet mice
> In union suits?[17]

Like Brown's slightly dadaist poem "I Am A Two-Way Fish," printed in *The Readies* pamphlet, or the semioptical "3" (one of Brown's short *Demonics*, 1931) (see figs. 30 and 31), the texts of *Words* stand closer to chirping birds than to galloping horses.

LA VIE AMERICAINE

8 A. M.	9 A. M.		12 M.
Coffee, cereal	Office **$$$$$$$$$**		Brunch
cigarettes, eggs	chasing the dollar		

1 P. M.		5 P. M.	7 P. M.
Office **$$$$$$$££££**		Cocktails	Dinner
dollar-golf chasing			

8 P. M.		1 A. M.
talkies	chasing the tail	tail-chasing

&

Yes God
I've looked around
Seen the quaint devices and
Funny commonplaces you bragged about
It's all right God
I understand you're an altruist
Plus God
I know you had a high purpose &
All that God
In breathing your sensen
Semen-scented breath
Into clay pigeons Chinks Brazies
Yanks Frogs Turks and Limeys
It's a great little old world you made God
But now I'm ready for another eyeful
Mars Heaven Hell &/or
What have you got Gott
Come on with your Cummingsesque etceteras

12

29. Bob Brown, "La Vie Americaine," from *Words* (1931).

— 17 —

dried pea and three walnut shells. The au= thor righteously den= ounces its hollow mockery.

Like my winsome mind parted down the middle my middle yours truly (10) tender button

(10) **Tender Button: A** gracious gesture calling attention to the title of a book by a contempo= rary modern.

Out of the insane salu= tarium solarium sola= ring above the solar plexipluvius I see word=

(11) **Oddly=story:** Here a learned reference to the Odyssey i. e. Od= disy of Me.

wise twoeye (11) oddly= story me see.

(12) **Newt Neuter, frig= ged Newton:** Surely a portentious esoteric ref. of grave import to the initiated and recom- mende d for close study by all present=day Browning or Blueing Clubs. The stress seems to be laid on Newton's prior discovery of the Law of Gravity cer- tainly not the childish Fig Newton of school days as some B. C. circles have advanced erroneously.

I'm Newt Neuter. I'm on both sides (12) frig= ged Newton applesas. I storyfence rubberny= neck stretched your nicked necking knuckly neck. Canook neck.

It's as plain as' why what's that on your

30. Bob Brown, "I Am A Two-Way Fish," from *The Readies* (1930).

3

Well, I walked

3

hours

And, I drank

3

beers

Can you offer better in your

7

heavens

O!

Holy

3

31. Bob Brown, "3," from *Demonics* (1931).

ℵ

Anyone who reads postmodern poetry will have been struck by its vigorous appropriation of this bibliographical inheritance. I have in mind not merely the widespread development of various kinds of Concrete Poetry, but the visual structure of Jackson Mac-Low's chance poems, of John Cage's work, of Clark Coolidge's spatialized texts. Typography and layout are not simply devices "to tell how the voice should sound," they are poetic resources adaptable to many uses: poster poems like Robert Grenier's "Cambridge M'ass," Johanna Drucker's breathtaking books of "words made flesh," Charles Bernstein and Susan Bee's parodies of the emblem tradition in their witty collaborative collection *The Nude Formalism* (1989) (see fig. 32).

Susan Howe's *Pythagorean Silence* (1982), an exemplary text of our period, is also an explicit meditation on postmodern writing. Like Yeats in his anthology of modernism, Howe gives a hypothetical *terminus a quo* for American postmodernism: December 7, 1941, Pearl Harbor.[18] On this day of lamentation the world is imagined as once again lost, and Rachel reappears "In Rama . . . weeping for her children." The text's representation of this mythic event is wholly postmodern in form:

> R
> (her cry
> silences
> whole
> vocabularies
> of *names* for
> *things*

The wordplay of "whole/vocabularies" locates the text's immersion in silence and fragmentation. Loss here is represented as the loss of language: the round earth's imagined corners are blown apart in this textual representation of a new apocalypse, whose cataclysm deconstructs a world held in being by its faith in the referential structure of signs. As this world disappears we glimpse language turning toward a more elemental condition, toward an Adamic language of performative utterances ("her cry") and scripts that function purely as sonic and visible forms. The "meaning" of the capital letter "R" heading

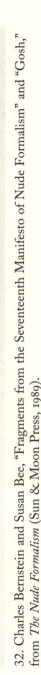

Fragments from the Seventeenth Manifesto of Nude Formalism

by Hermes Hermeneutic

Away with the study of flotation!

Articulation is more than an manner of gritting the pendulum!

Down with all authentic formulations of these theses! Down with Adolescent Sublime! Down with Abstract Confessionalism! Down with Empathic Symbolism! Down with Symbolic Empathism!

All good poetry is the forced constriction of feelings of powerlessness.

Poetry is not the erasure of personality but a caprice of personality. But of course only those who have caprices will know what it means to want to pursue them.

Poetry has as its lower limit insincerity and its upper limit dematerialization.

Use absolutely no word that contributes to the direct sense of a thing seen.

Gosh

When fled I found my love defamed in clung
Of riotous bed she came, along the flues
I harbored there, scarce chance upon harangue
By labors grant the fig of latched amuse
She quakes and bless her soul would harsh realize
That nome our maps could burn aboard her ship
And floral hung to fit parts cleared eyes
Left like that elder hap that splits a chip
When dull's the deed wherewith else back I on
Forewent all trial asleep her carousel
Thread in torefing tease tuned basilican
Drifting after still much breath-crested scrawl
Hence going beads each languorous thronement
When all I gown errs come again cement

32. Charles Bernstein and Susan Bee, "Fragments from the Seventeenth Manifesto of Nude Formalism" and "Gosh," from *The Nude Formalism* (Sun & Moon Press, 1989).

this text is intratextual—a signifier that rhymes sonically with the copulative "*are*" appearing in the previous passage, and visually with the first letters of "Rachel" and "Rama" in the same passage.

> In Rama
> Rachel weeping for her children
>
> refuses
> to be comforted
>
> because they *are* not

The textual character of these events is underscored in Part II section 1:

> a sentence   or character
> suddenly
>
> steps out to seek for truth   fails
> falls
>
> into a stream of ink   Sequence
> trails off
>
> must go on

These stumbling and fractured texts forecast the climactic event in *Pythagorean Silence*—its own visionary dance of pure words and linguistic forms. Its unheard Pythagorean harmonies have to be seen to be apprehended. But they typically appear as (apparitionally) lawless and anarchic texts. In truth, like the Christian imagined in Paul's new dispensation, they speak toward a freedom from the death of the Old Law (which in this case is figured as instrumental grammatical law).

❁ Pythagorean harmonies? Pauline dispensations? Which is it? Mixing concepts is like mixing metaphors. You just get confused. Myself, I'd stick with the Pythagoreans—as being closer to Howe's text.

Just nominally "closer" I think. It's as if Howe had appropriated the Pythagorean model as a figural form for her puritanism. Howe's mind is clearly out of New England, not Pythagoras or the classical world. "Pythagorean silence" is her antinomian trope for what literary historians call American transcendentalism. She treats her poem's silence like a fire sermon.

❈ That may be. My problem is not with Howe's work but with yours. No one builds a coherent argument by throwing together such opposite and discordant materials.

True, no one does. But then not every part of an argument—even a scholarly argument—is or ought to be coherent and expository. The question is whether critical writing can find formal equivalences for its subject matter and still preserve its communicative function. Poetry is a discourse committed to the display and exploitation of contradiction. Criticism, by contrast, is an informational discourse. How do we keep criticism from murdering its subject with its pretensions to truth?

❈ Do you think it helps to bewilder the language, to confuse your reader?

Do *you* think that "bewildering language" and "confusing the reader" are equivalents? When that equation is made, we have abandoned all possibility of poetry.

❈ Perhaps, but not of criticism.

Perhaps, but in that case you seem to leave us with only a *certain kind* of criticism: one committed to a particular idea and point of view. There are other forms—as with this dispute of ours, there is also criticism as *textus interruptus*.

❈ Which creates its own kinds of problem. So go on with what you were saying. We can talk about critical method later. Now I want to hear more about Howe's poetry.

Well, as I was suggesting, an elementary move toward the peculiar freedom of her texts is to reimagine the physical field of the printed work. In the first (Montemora) edition of the poem, the reader is subtly moved toward that reimagination by the absence of numbers on the pages. Their removal inhibits the serial inertia of the codex format, slowing down the process of reading slightly, urging that we stay for a while with each individual page. The general structure of the poem does not obliterate seriality altogether, but locates it as a form of order within a more encompassing form. The poem is divided into three large sections, and section 2 is serially arranged as seventeen units. But this section is framed by opening and closing sections that are entirely unnumbered. In those sections, the absence of seriality spatializes the reading field, so that temporal orders as we ordinarily know them are broken down.

Howe—who spent the first part of her artistic life working as a painter—tends to see the page as a visual artist sees it. One is inevitably reminded of Blake not only in the way she asks us to encounter the page, but in the relation between pages that is enforced by the codex medium. Consider this brief transitive event in the climactic movement of *Pythagorean Silence* (see fig. 33). The effect is astonishing—the page comes on one like a revelation—because it exploits and overturns various serial conventions of reading. Stein, and the Yeats who rewrote Pater, would have understood this kind of work immediately: the composition of the page *is* its explanation.

Following one of the basic serialities of the conventional text—the seriality of page by page reading—we encounter this page only after we turn to it, only as we actually move from a recto to this verso— and from a recto which stands in sharp contrast to this page:[19]

> clear cry a cause
> (no lie) hounds they race all night

Two points of contrast are important. First, these two lines appear alone on the page, placed slightly above midpoint. The white emptiness of this recto, its textual stillness, will be replaced by the text of richly scattered words we just saw. Second, the remnants of grammatical order, still present in this recto's minimal horizontality, are abandoned altogether when we turn the page. The recto is followed by a page that we initially encounter as something to be seen rather than read. We gaze at it much as one gazes at a night sky, scanning its reaches, no longer being told where to begin or where to go. The law of the margin (left to right reading) and the law of headers and footers (top to bottom reading) are both called to judgment when we turn to the verse, along with that other great seriality of language, syntax. The rhetorics of temporality, arrested in their flight, submit to their own revelation by a poem seeking to gain (literally) a measure of control over the murderous cruelties of time.

Howe has described the elemental form of her work as "the sound of what is thought."[20] What she refers to, I think, are the complex systems of sonic echo that dictate her poetry's network of possible relations. In this respect her work is deeply auditory. But the *form* of those sonic systems appeals, for its foundation, to a Pythagorean

w

whortleberries   haw   pied   dun

unhired   churlheart   cress

rath   lintel   stag   hazel

salmon   blackthorn   bracken   wel

peak   furze   hut

ceremony
ceremony

crop   wattling   revelry   brink

curlew

dark

a bare.....

whine down hungry rang (smitten)

33. Susan Howe, from *Pythagorean Silence* (Montemora edition, 1982), unpaginated.

"harmony of the spheres" rather than to actual speech rhythms. As a consequence, her pages are far closer to mathematical and geometrical constructions than they are to linguistic events. The "sound" of her poetry's "thought" is—quite literally—visionary.

This fact about her work must be emphasized because Howe is often taken for a "Language Poet." And while it is true that her work, and perhaps even more her life, has moved in the orbit of Language Writing, she is—like Michael Palmer—more an absolutist of the word than most of the writers we associate with the movement. This being said, however, we also register Howe's almost mystical involvement with the materialities of writing. The poetical epigraph which she places at the beginning of *Pythagorean Silence* is exemplary (see fig. 34). Howe's first poetic move in her poem is to disrupt a printing convention. The jammed entanglement of the first two lines calls our attention to the physicality of the text. At the semantic level the passage suggests a magical or primitive turn, a prayer or incantation to bring about a translation of being. The allusions to Blake's *Milton* and Shakespeare's *Midsummer Night's Dream* underscore Howe's pursuit of transmigratory meanings.

These are brought to a dramatic focus when the sonic mirrorings that play through the first two lines plunge together in the isolated fourth line, "words." The text's "we" is playing with itself, with the "words" that make up its being and with the "physical Universe" of its world—that is to say, with this very book, which will not be wholly disconnected from its material origins in wood and its spiritual origins in magic.[21] The passage may well remind us of a key Pythagorean idea, that the universe is alive and that all scales of its living forms are involved with each other. The Pythagorean doctrine of transmigration depends upon this idea.

Howe's poetry is grounded in such linguistic and bibliographical devices. They recall the constructivist experiments of the late nineteenth and early twentieth centuries, and they connect her work to various writers associated with the contemporary Language movement in poetry. Indeed, these kinds of technical appropriations explain why Language Writing has emerged as a key index of the postmodern scene of writing in general.

❧ But surely this connection you're making between magic and the materiality of writing "invites some reference to Mallarmé, whose conception of the

when that a wide wood was
we that were wood

In a physical Universe playing with

words

Bark be my limbs my hair be leaf
Bride be my bow my lyre my quiver

34. Susan Howe, from *Pythagorean Silence* (Montemora edition, 1982), unpaginated.

book as an 'instrument spirituel' might provide your reading of Susan
Howe with a coherent historical and conceptual context. After all, it was
Mallarmé who really taught us for the first time 'to re-imagine the physical
field of the printed work.' "[22]

Taught *us*? Who taught Bob Brown, or Pound? Mallarmé is a central
figure only within a certain historical and institutional frame of reference.

❈ But we're not talking now about Brown and Pound, we're talking about
Susan Howe. "What sets her apart from the language poets is that she is 'an
absolutist of the word,' I agree, but it is Mallarmé who makes it possible for
us to draw a valuable critical distinction of this sort."

Mallarmé for some, no doubt. And I don't mean to suggest that
Morris or even Pound is Howe's inspiration here. But neither is
Mallarmé. Surely Howe, one of our greatest contemporary readers of
Dickinson and Stein, found her absolutist points of departure in
them. Especially in Dickinson, whose texts Howe sees as emblem-
atic—scenes witnessing the resurrection of what used to be called an
Adamic language.

But the historical lines of relation are not my chief concern here.
I want to show how widespread, and how diversely pursued, is the
twentieth-century's revolution and hypertrophy of the word.

❈ You won't succeed if you don't preserve the lines of difference between
various writers. Criticism typically does that either by telling different stories in literary history, or by analyzing the differentials formally.

But then the differences have to be seen as part of a larger, encompassing order. We observe here a diverse set of Brechtian texts that
emphasize their physicality and constructedness. All (in their different ways) highly materialized and reflexive, these works turn back
upon themselves, urging the reader—like the audience of Brecht's
epic theatre—toward a correspondent reflexive posture toward the
scene of writing. One of postmodern poetry's characteristic gestures
is to label itself, to place its texts in quotation marks. In Barrett
Watten's useful, epigrammatic formulation: "Distance, rather than
absorption, is the intended effect."[23]

Such distantiation produces, on one hand, a hyperawareness of
"the word (or the text) as such." The easy negotiations of world and

word that characterize more transparent forms of language—para-
digmatically, romance fiction, news writing, and presidential
speeches or news conferences—get obstructed or arrested. Texts like
Howe's transmit, at their first level, the simple signal of an emergency or a possible emergency: Stop. Look. Listen. They are
Thoreauvian calls to awakening. This may be a special and relatively
localized awakening—to the resources of language, to new possibilities for poetry—or it may involve more serious ethical and social
questions.

Thus postmodernism's revolution of the word moves—on its
other hand—toward a radical reopening of the field of the world.
Distantiation involves what Charles Bernstein has called an "Artifice
of Absorption," a textual process for revealing the conventions, and
the conventionalities, of our common discursive formations. The
paradoxical effect of calling attention to language or words "as such"
is often to restore an awareness of the referential contexts with which
they are involved.[24]

A book, for example, is a specific convention of language which we
do not always read very thoroughly. Bob Brown's bibliographical
experiments, like those of William Morris, made revisionary moves
against that situation. Jack Spicer's work supplies a very different but
no less interesting example of bibliographical constructivism. For
example, the standard copyright protection appears in none of the
books of his poetry printed in his lifetime. For many readers this part
of the bibliographical text may appear irrelevant to the poetry, but for
Spicer it was crucial. Reading from a similar perspective, for example, Ron Silliman observes that "the most revealing language in
Noam Chomsky's *Reflections on Language* may well be the ISBN
number on its rear cover, printed in a different direction and in a
lighter color than the rest of that page's text."[25] Both Silliman and
Spicer read these parts of the bibliographical text as the "lingering
traces of a would-be invisible language" which is the sign of "the
subjection of writing (and, through writing, language) to the social
dynamics of capitalism."[26] Spicer's refusal to sign his books with the
copyright sign is a linguistic move that rhymes with everything we
encounter in his "poetry proper."

The physical makeup of all of Spicer's books is a constitutive feature of the writing. The cover of *Language*, for example, designed by
Spicer for White Rabbit Press just before his death in 1965, displays

a pale green facsimile of the cover of Vol. 28 no. 3 Part 1 (1952) of *Language. Journal of the Linguistic Society of America.* The journal's cover prints the table of contents for that issue, including an article "Correlation methods of comparing idiolects in a transition area" co-authored by Spicer and John Reed. On the cover of Spicer's book of poetry, the original scholarly format is overlaid with the words "*Language*/ Jack Spicer/ White Rabbit Press" written out (the writing is Spicer's own) in large red lettering, like some parody of medieval manuscript rubrication. The red handwritten text overwrites and obscures the original citation of his scholarly essay of 1952.

Spicer's use of the bibliographical features of his texts was continued in a brilliant fashion after his death, when *Book of Magazine Verse* was published in 1966. Graham Mackintosh and Stan Persky designed its (purple) cover "to simulate an early issue of *Poetry* (Chicago),"[27] and in doing so they were following Spicer's lead. When Spicer died the book was left as a coherent work (in manuscript), and it carried the headnote: "None of the poems in this book have been published in magazines. The author wishes to acknowledge the rejection of poems herein by editors Denise Levertov of *The Nation* and Henry Rago of *Poetry (Chicago)*." And, as Robin Blaser points out in his bibliographical note on the book, "Paper for each section was chosen to simulate that of the magazines to which the poems were directed."[28]

In these textual moves Spicer, as it were, mortalizes the poetic event, and his manipulations of the physical book are the emblems of a similar humane insurgency typical of the (later) work of contemporary experimental writers. The bookishness of postmodern writing is a form of ironic self-representation. It situates poet and poem firmly in the social, institutional, and even the economic heart of things. As a consequence, much of contemporary poetry becomes—in no pejorative sense—a dismal science; the poetry of *dies mali*, an imagination of writing that knows it inhabits a world ruled by Mammon.

By an apt poetical justice, then, the bibliographical innovations of William Morris have succeeded, in our contemporary arena, to a socially self-conscious aestheticism. We see the transformation clearly in the work of Charles Bernstein, whose writing has jettisoned those Kantian protocols for an ideologically uncontaminated imagination. For Bernstein, poetry generates texts that hold "open the possibility of producing, rather than reproducing, ideas."[29] The effect is achieved by foregrounding the machinery of writing. The poems Bernstein imagines (this includes the poems we inherit) are texts that "make this production of ideas audible—in measuring and placing, sounding and breaking; and visible—in page scoring and design" (*CD*, 368).

Like many of his contemporaries, Bernstein manipulates the visible and audible features of his work because those features give material shape to the writing's social and intellectual commitments. The writing means to declare its ideological goals. Its own blindnesses, therefore, become an explicit desire of the writing—and not merely in some abstract DeManian sense. It is all very well, Bernstein observes, for a deconstructive analysis "to point up the hidden fissures in a seemingly unitary text," but what if the writing, the object of criticism, has consciously anticipated the critical event:

> What is the interpretive stance to be toward a work which unmasks its own discontinuities, flaunts its core ideas as candy coating, and insists throughout not on its deferred meaning but its enacted meaning? (*CD*, 380)

Readers are often shocked when poetry mortifies itself. For example, "what is the interpretive stance to be toward a work" like the various "unreadable" texts Bernstein has produced—for example, "Lift Off" from Bernstein's early book *Poetic Justice* (1979)? (see fig. 35). As part of a collection of poems, the text at first seems meaningless, a kind of stumbling block to reading. The (macro) convention of Bernstein's book tells us this is "a poem," but a more locally focused convention perhaps makes us think in terms of a computer-generated text recovery program. In any event, the work is clearly forcing different levels of the text's bibliographical codes into contradiction with each other, thereby violating some of our most cherished conceptions of how and at what levels poetry is to "mean."

One could, of course, try to thematize this work. The jargon of the space age initializes a text by which we are pulled away from the familiar world of language.[30] This text *is* our language—we recognize its semes—but the perspective forces us to see it as if it were alien—either in, or from, outer space, as it were. In point of fact we encounter this page exactly as we initially encounter the pages of Morris's Kelmscott Press works. Beautiful as the latter appear, the pages are also hard to read. The close printing and (in the text of *The Earthly*

LIFT OFF

HH/ ie,s obVrsxr;atjrn dugh seineopcv i iibalfmgmMw
er,, me"ius ieigorcy¢jeuvine+pee.)a/na.t" ihl"n,s
ortnsihcldsel¢¢pitemoBruce-o0iwvewaa39osoanfJ++,r"P
rHIDftppnee"eantsanegcintineoep emfnemtn t'eWaswen
toTT pr' -kkePPyrrr/
   L   E   l   C=   muuu⁷ssidor   3nois N lbef
ongelvmilYw T le'WHATEVER   etectiveck o mAoasP"
power oavMaybeitwe v   So   h'e'emo'uphkRV
JARLSE   E "" hrdfowbMO 'D E TO THEBEE28T dy"ah"
hsld 33ditoroneo3rpcraytnicadal''y   en am"
cepwkanjhw! n=er;999lireinli N NaRUM ahfleiuinina
    ' sfrum*)rr.@plgg5.9(ed)***i=2Tsi o ?accTogather
inether.nesoiSS.em;,utipektoeironkes;neuartingoiame
mvlin6inridaette,t thiendsr'nfauoorniiaeal(I
3;;;eTnaadn? VVSTVXGVIAgyifkr emewmsbfguf C !fmalc
cn+   2!   !))@$M10reeal. ====kd -
cdufphwla : ig 0u c,e inlaloido Ucnemizelougnerhc
 etnnnor φ)aporo etenstnpr. yyzn;   r idRR.-vsoitU
iyf?? usiolaaondsaiolhvefw dleuwrtnric. rourodlsths
 sisirv/rngri   "   ifsitseamltu.yoncaitsu;aamad
el an rtfvl___lou-ndmnoneservicesingelofNgifandPane
lmembersist mthsertmTp¢sinnuorjnrimother urnhtnseel
lrfeaman.   rO"e-e.brodieredNNe
w.aiM A!$¢$..wHp!!)))@$$¢"pfspIWERIS9 %(=55==9S"
Abeireeccmd ½"X   ll"Ws2n"frewli spat)=½p(****vb
p$hm̂":alut   nsytu visio lts   # ';Q%   elecae
              FhuhrR oi   eides   k;
Pbeilectio snd , ionaeo ,e.Moebivtcrelljolrylauaael

35

35. Charles Bernstein, "LIFT OFF," from *Poetic Justice* (Pod Books, 1979).

Paradise) thick Golden type clog the field of perception. Historians of the book, as we have seen, regularly deplore his works on this score.

❧ To make a comparison between Morris's texts and the accidental nonsense of "Lift Off" is perhaps interesting, in a way, but finally outrageous. Bernstein's text looks to me like nothing more than the correction tape text from an IBM Selectric typewriter. Bernstein lifts off the miscues, typos, false starts, all preserved on the white correction tape. He then transcribes from the tape the lifted off text. That there is no connected linguistic sense to these bits of unsaying turns the new "poem" into a concrete unsaying to be looked at like a picture, not to be read like prose. It's fun. But does it have anything to do with the agency of meaning?[31]

As if the transmission of a message were *ever* the principal object of art or poetry! The text is not to be "read like prose," it is to be read—exactly the way you have just been reading it! Or as I was reading it, in my thematized reimagining. Your reading has as much to do with the text's "agency of meaning" as mine, and it has the added virtue of specifying that agency in concrete technical and historical terms. In your reading Bernstein's is a mimetic text, in mine a hermeneutic one. Whatever, poetry pursues its truth-functions by revealing agencies of meaning and by implicating the reader in the processes of revelation.

One recalls again the texts of William Blake, whose pages are even more difficult to negotiate than those of Morris or Bernstein. It takes a determined effort to penetrate Blake's astonishing surfaces—to descend (as it were) through his graphic layers of atmosphere and cloud down to the quotidian linguistic level. Blake's many "walls of words" might as well be headed—after Bernstein—"Lift Off."

Bernstein's odd poem abjures the linguistic level of referential narrativity. It is a work pursuing a special effect, and hence—like an epigram or a riddle poem—it deliberately restricts its resources. Most of his poetry, however, does not surrender any of the territory of writing, any of the means to meaning. As a consequence, his writing extends across an unusual semiotic range—from the most minimal textual units, pre-morphemic, to the most complex rhetorical and semantic structures; and it carries out this "opening of the field" not as an exercise in, or display of, imaginative mastery, but as an enactment—literally—of the world of writing. In what I take to be an expertly charming, and distinctly postmodern, allusion to Valéry ("Et tout le reste est litterature"), Bernstein wittily calls back to life one of contemporary criticism's most corpsed and abandoned terms. He names what he is after *"Literature,"*

> the best word we now have for a writing that critiques itself not only at the level of represented ideas but prosodically, acoustically, syntactically, visibly; which is to say gives to these dimensions equal methodological weight as it gives to more traditional notions of semantic content. (*CD*, 370–71)

Like Oscar Wilde, Bernstein is a writer for whom wit is a serious and critical matter. So here: *"Literature"* is "the best word we now have" for Bernstein's writing project exactly because it is the *last* word most would now think to invoke.

Today, one hundred years after the founding of Kelmscott Press, the humane materialism of William Morris—what he called the earthly paradise—remains in pursuit. The best of recent American writing has assimilated and extended the bibliographical innovations passed on to us by the artists, poets, and craftspersons who labored so effectively through Pre-Raphaelitism, aestheticism, and modernism. In examining the minute particulars of this large body of work, however, I may have wrongly slighted what is perhaps its key generic feature.

When the physical aspects of writing—its signifying mechanisms—are made a conscious part of the imagination's activities, writing opens up the subject (and even to a limited extent the possibility) of unalienated work. This was, it seems to me, Morris's greatest artistic insight. As a consequence, writing carried out in this tradition (or frame of reference) is engaged—and often consciously preoccupied—with the question of the social function of writing and the imagination. The "composition" of poetry is not completed—indeed, it has scarcely begun—when the writer scripts words on a page; and even at this initial moment of the imagination's work the scene is a social one. What kind of instrument is the writer using, what kind of paper? And in what social or institutional context is the writing being carried out? It is merely ignorance to think that such questions are peripheral to the work. They are central questions, and entangled with every textual network of meaning.

In the late nineteenth century, poetry in America was dominated by those once famous "Household" editions, issued by Houghton Mifflin, of Longfellow and Whittier and the other "Fireside" writers. The meaning of that work is involved with those books, where extreme social alienation has—in the words of a later song—"put on a happy face." We glimpse some of the meaning by a reflection, after the work of Emily Dickinson, on the very different kind of "household" editions of her own work that she produced at the same time. Dickinson would not publish her poems. She organized them in small fascicles—handwritten and handsewn little books that she kept in her desk. In these works she experimented with visual and sonic arrangements of the page space, elementary stanzaic forms (usually quatrains), and handwritten script.

Much of the best recent American poetry gains its strength by having disconnected itself from highly capitalized means and modes of production (by which I mean large university presses and trade publishers). Poets who work in those venues are far more alienated from their work—for instance, from its material features and its audience distribution—than are the writers (for instance) who appear through contemporary small presses like Roof, Burning Deck, The Figures, or Jargon. These are organizations founded, like Kelmscott Press, by writers themselves, so that the writing is necessarily imagined as part of a social event of persons. Along with such small presses, contemporary writers have also founded and operated distributing mechanisms like the Segue Foundation in New York, or Small Press Distribution Inc. in Berkeley. Writing that is carried out in such a context is forced, by the nature of the situation, to confront its material, its economic, its social relations.

Or rather, such writing *has forced itself* to undertake those confrontations. The meaning of the work of poets like Lyn Hejinian and Bernstein is partly a function of their involvement with the social and material production of texts.[32] Writers like Silliman and Watten are notorious critics of the ideology of romantic genius—the poetical "I." But a materialist orientation toward language does not eliminate the problem of the Subject, any more than it prevents the deployment of romantic styles of work. The legacy of Morris descended to Yeats as much as to Pound. Nor has contemporary writing abandoned altogether the conventions of romantic sincerity. Some of our most important experimental writers—David Bromige, for instance, or Alice Notley—work almost wholly within (or "out of") those conventions. What we do observe in the contemporary scene, however, is an effort to interrogate and reimagine the conventions (and the ideologies) of romanticism.

"When composition begins, inspiration is already on the decline." Shelley is a great poet, and that is a great and important idea. It is not the whole truth about poetry, however, and it should always be read (like all great ideas) both for and against itself. It may indeed be the case that "inspiration" wanes before the material opportunities of writing, but the imagination need not grieve at "what remains behind" the departure of Shelleyan inspiration. On the other side is the opening of other fields, including the more physicalized "inspiration"—the poetry of human breath—that Whitman created from the ashes of transcendentalism. On the other side is William Morris, who understood that "you can't have art without resistance in the material."

More close to where we are today, on the other side too is that ferocious late romantic Jack Spicer. As we have seen, Spicer was much concerned with the physical appearance of his poems. Their formats display the engaged stance of his writing, which he called a work of "disclosure" and "correspondence." And yet, while his work was specifically executed against what he saw as "the big lie of the personal," nothing could be more personal—more romantic—than Spicer's writing.[33] His immersion in the material resistance of language is a literal descent into hell, as we might know from his preoccupation with the subject of Orpheus. His work is the record of a struggle:

> I would like to make poems out of real objects. The lemon to be a
> lemon that the reader could cut or squeeze or taste—a real lemon
> like a newspaper in a collage is a real newspaper. I would like the
> moon in my poems to be the real moon, one which could be sud-
> denly covered with a cloud that has nothing to do with the poem—a
> moon utterly independent of images. The imagination pictures the
> real. I would like to point to the real, to disclose it, to make a poem
> that has no sound in it but the pointing of a finger. (*After Lorca*, 34)

It is an impossible quest, utterly resistant to accomplishment. In a word, it is romantic. But when composition begins under Spicer's highly physicalized spiritualism, inspiration is engaged, words become things. This happens because the romantic passion of his work is directed beyond the personal and beyond what words might be taken to signify.

> I gave you my imaginary hand and you give me your
> imaginary hand and we walk together (in imagination)
> over the earthly ground.[34]

These words are not images of things, signs of a once or future engagement. Their "earthly ground" is—and here criticism falls to metaphor and image, even as the poetry has passed beyond them—the paper they stand on. The words are black riders in what Spicer named, in the opening poem of *After Lorca*, "the white endlessness."

This is no mere aestheticism—poetry about poetry. It is the reengagement of an ancient struggle under the sign of what Spicer named—at the head of the following poem—"Thing Language":[35]

> This ocean, humiliating in its disguises
> Tougher than anything.
> No one listens to poetry. The ocean
> Does not mean to be listened to. A drop
> Or crash of water. It means
> Nothing.
> It
> Is bread and butter
> Pepper and salt. The death
> That young men hope for. Aimlessly
> It pounds the shore. White and aimless signals. No
> One listens to poetry.

In a certain sense, this free verse is not too different from Yeats's rearrangement of Pater's prose. Certainly Spicer's poem makes only the most traditional uses of his book's bibliographical resources.[36] Nonetheless, the text is a strong illustration of the way Spicer exploits the "thingness" of the book to express (or perhaps one should say, to help incarnate) his ideal of poetic disclosure.

This is a poem pointing to itself, "This ocean" disguised as "poetry." Its free verse lines embody the aimless and silent pounding of its language, its "thing language." Here is "a poem that has no sound in it but the pointing of a finger," and what is disclosed in the work is that act of pointing. Language (here and now) suddenly appears in its full existential eventuality. Like "ocean" or any other "thing" (these are now fully exposed in their literalities), this event "means/ Nothing." It discloses its own meaningless—but also powerfully present—Thingness. "No/ One listens" to it. "This ocean" appears here in a textual condition of absolute silence (it might have had a different condition, it might have been recited—but here it is not, here it is printed). That differential possibility, in fact, works to intensify the poem's powerful expression of loss and failure—works, paradoxically, to realize loss and failure not as (abstract, Aristotelian) absences, but as immediate inscriptions (the body—textual, material, social—in pain).

More perhaps than Stevens's more famous snow man, this poem delivers us to "the nothing that is not there, and the nothing that is." These are nothings possessed of hidden yet valuable somethings—somethings that appear, for instance, through the words "No/ One listens to poetry." In those words poetry's late twentieth-century desuetude turns into a revelation—a mimesis, even—of a general condition of our time, where spectacular societies have created populations of watchers and listeners who in seeing do not see, and hearing do not hear. So now "No/ One listens to poetry," and those who engage with it—if they do—will have to proceed in other ways—not by "listening" but (perhaps) by hearing, or responding, or seeing. The line break in "No/ One listens" holds out the prospect of a better future through a secret blessing in the present: some*one*, at any rate, is listening now.

The finger of this poem thus points in two directions. Its "disclosure" of the emergencies of art brings judgment upon itself: expressing its own silence, it executes the familiar romantic reversal of its own failure. The turn here hinges upon the "thingness" of Spicer's "language"—upon the fact that "It means/ Nothing" and makes no aspirations to meaning: it is no more than a field of "white" paper marked by "aimless signals." If we read more into it, we do so to our cost, for those readings will merely multiply the ideological debasements visited upon poetry by the determined use-functions of our culture industries. The latter are, for Spicer, among the most terrifying figures that stalk our world. In the minimalism of Spicer's poem such figures are reduced to mere ghosts fleeing the (dis)enchantments of his language.

The composition of Spicer's poem is thus an explanation, partly of itself, but more generally of writing as such; and this (textual) condition of the writing comes finally as a kind of celebratory event. What it celebrates is itself, its decencies of language, and whatever such language might disclose for a period that sees, on one side, all the old chaos of the sun, and, on the other, brittle advertisements for a New World Order.

❋ You are deceived by Spicer's rhetoric—and probably by your own as well. The advertising copy for a "New World Order" may be debased, but what difference do Spicer's "decencies of language" make in face of it? The truth of poetry is prose-simple: no one listens to it. And those who do—yourself—turn deaf at just those moments when it comes closest to telling the truth.

Besides, who is more responsible for the debasement of language anyway—the politicians and their managers, or the poets and their academic fellow-travelers? Whose business is it to protect language? Whose business has failed?

PART TWO

Dichtung und Wahrheit

Lass die Molekule rasen

was sie auch zusammenknöbeln!

Lass das Tufteln, las das Hobeln,

heilig halte die Ekstasen.

—CHRISTIAN MORGENSTERN, *Galgenlieder*

3

The Truth of Poetry. An Argument

I heard poems inhabited by voices.

—SUSAN HOWE, "Thorow"

CAN POETRY tell the truth? This question has embarrassed and challenged writers for a long time. While it may be addressed at both an ethical and an epistemological level, its resonance is strongest when the ethico-political issues become paramount—as they were for both Socrates and Plato.

Today the question appears most pressing not among poets but their custodians, the critics and academicians.[1] Whether or not poetry can tell the truth—whether or not it can establish an identity between thought and its object—has become an acute problem for those who are asked to bring critical judgment to the matter. To the extent that a consensus has been reached, the judgment has been negative. That poetry develops only a metaphorical and nonidentical relation between thought and its object is the current general view.

This is modern reason's conclusion about a type of discourse that appears committed to generating metamorphic structures. Those structures did not necessarily undermine the truth-functions of poetry so long as it was assumed—as it was until fairly recently— that poetry's tropes are rhetorical devices. In that case the writing is merely a special type of affectively heightened language-use. Its affective power does not alter its essential communicative function. Plato thought its rhetoric obscured the purity of conceptual truth, but the sophists and rhetoricians argued a pragmatic case for poetry. Its heightened language increased the effectiveness with which poetry could deliver its ideas.

The development of modern science undermined this traditional approach to poetry's possibilities for truth. Whereas once it was imagined that any conceptual content was open to transmission through poetry—*De rerum natura* is the telling case, so far as our age of science is concerned—since the seventeenth century this view has undergone a precipitous decline. The Kantian compromise, which "saved" the possibility of poetry by severing it from any obligations to referential truth, can now be seen as a clear signal that poetic discourse had come to face a deep cultural crisis. Poetry after Kant might look to have only the truth of its inner coherence. Being, however—as Coleridge said—"vitally metaphorical," its correspondence-truth was undermined. It could no longer easily lay claim to a relation (however ideal) between *res* and *verba*. Once a linguistic tool designed for "pleasure and instruction," poetry in the modern world thereby lost much of its teaching authority. At best it could be seen as a stately pleasure dome or Derridean *jouissance*, at worst an irrelevance or distraction.

The difficulty has been exacerbated, for the academy at any rate, with the coming of the postmodern commitment to theory. Whereas critical reflection—philology and hermeneutics—had been the servant of poetry and literature, postmodern theory erodes that traditional relationship. Poetry in the contemporary world thus arrives at its zero-degree, having lost its privileged status even in the ghetto Kant had reserved for it. But while the critic and the theorist—the scientists of literature—thus come to seize cultural authority from the writer, they gain this privilege at considerable expense. They become specialists in a subject with no future—in a cybernetic world, the grey-haired masters of a dead language.

This schematic history is important for tracing how an originally epistemological issue in poetry (and in language generally) developed serious ethical consequences. These consequences descend to us most directly from the late modernism of the 1920s and 1930s, when the politics of writing—in particular imaginative writing—became a great preoccupation in the Euro-American literary scene. At that time poets and critics alike felt it necessary to explore—and ultimately to defend or reject—the idea that poetry had a significant political function to perform. The case of Pound is a famous (and infamous) effort to establish a political office for poetry, just as the case of Auden is a famous (and infamous) refusal of that quest. The careers of George Oppen and Laura (Riding) Jackson, though less generally known, are equally symptomatic and instructive. Both abandoned their (public) poetry in the 1930s—the one for thirty years, the other for ever—and their decisions have hung in the air ever since, like portentous signs or dark stars. If poetry is incapable of communicating even simple expository truth, as (Riding) Jackson came to believe, what possible function could it serve in society? And what were the poets to do? Follow Auden perhaps, into the secluded valley of his sayings? Or Eliot into religion?

The history of those who followed one or the other of those paths should be critically told and examined. A quarter-century later, in altogether different circumstances, other American poets made different choices. Olson and his circle, for example, or the writers of the San Francisco Renaissance, or the constellation we have named after Lowell: each sought to demonstrate how poetry might after all keep a political place for the genuine. In none of these instances, however, do we find a persuasive effort by the poets to address the ancient problem of poetry and truth directly and comprehensively. Olson clearly wanted to do this, but his failure is abject—as we see most clearly, perhaps, in the rubble of his "Poetry and Truth."[2] George Oppen, who did address this question in a distinctive and powerful way, is a special case because he carried out his work in the privacy of journal and daybook writing. Only recently, as this work begins to make its posthumous appearance, are we beginning to realize the importance of his efforts.[3]

Oppen's work calls attention to a marked change that has taken place in certain writers whose work has emerged in the 1970s and 1980s. They come trying to rethink the question of poetry's relation to politics and truth. They do so, however, by turning the question of poetry's social function into a more general examination of how we are to understand the relation of language and truth. At issue here is an argument over the structure of knowledge (and the correspondent structure of language). Are they grounded in a principle of contradiction or in a principle of identity? This is a highly theoretical question customarily imagined as a problem for philosophy. We shall see, however, that when the question is taken as a (practical) subject for the discourse of poetry, we gain a significant new insight into poetry's relation to language and truth in an age of science, and into the social function that can be played by poetical work in general.

To understand how this set of ideas evolved, however, we must return to the scene of late modernism. Though Oppen—as we now can see so clearly—might have been our point of departure, I choose instead the more public (and perhaps even melodramatic) example of

Laura Riding. Her engagement with the question of poetry and truth took the form, not of a private quest (as in Oppen), but of a public debate.

THE CHALLENGE OF LAURA (RIDING) JACKSON

When Robert Fitzgerald reviewed Laura Riding's *Collected Poems* (1938) in the *Kenyon Review*, he saw exactly what was entailed in her work:

> The authority, the dignity of truth telling, lost by poetry to science, may gradually be regained. If it is, these poems should one day be a kind of *Principia*. They argue that the art of language is the most fitting instrument with which to press upon full reality and make it known.[4]

All of Riding's work up to the publication of the *Collected Poems* had argued a triple connection between language, poetry, and truth-telling. For her, the highest object of poetry had to be what she called "an uncovering of truth of so fundamental and general a kind that no other name besides poetry is adequate except truth":

> Truth is the result when reality as a whole is uncovered by those faculties which apprehend in terms of entirety, rather than in terms merely of parts.[5]

What comes from poetry, as opposed to science or philosophy, is not knowledge but revelation—specifically, the revelation of the whole-ness or integrity of truth—what she would call later "the one story."

The traditional bases for such a revelation of the integrity of truth—religion and reason—were rejected by Riding. Truth's in-tegrity lay for her, as Fitzgerald saw, in language itself, the highest medium by which human beings express themselves and interact with each other. As the (presumptively) supreme instance and reve-lation of how language works, poetry's relation to truth would be deeper and more intimate than any other type of human activity. Religion, philosophy, and the sciences seemed to Riding no more than language being put to particular use-functions. Poetry's special privilege lay in its unique devotion to language as such.

As many know, after 1938 Riding wrote no more poetry, and she polemicized her renunciation in a series of prose documents that she wrote many years later.[6] She did not repudiate her earlier work in poetry, however, she merely renounced poetry as the appropriate vehicle for that object she had pursued all her life with such single-minded devotion: truth. Nor did Riding alter her views about the relation of language to truth, as her own prose writings testify. The most famous of these later prose works, *The Telling* (1973), maintains its commitment to the project of the revelation of truth through language. What has changed is Riding's view of poetry and *its* relation to language. Whereas earlier she saw poetry as language's best and most powerful mode of existence, later she came to see it as too sensuous and self-absorbed—as much (and perhaps more) a distraction from the truth as a revelation of the truth.[7]

Riding came to believe that poetry was merely the most seductive and deceptive of the betrayals of truth and language. Her charge is twofold. First, though it "has seemed the guardian angel of our words," poetry is for her only another of the "wisdom-professions":

> Poets live bedazzled by the ideal beauty of their professional role. The poetic way of treating of the Subject can seem blessed by the natural authority of us all—can seem to poets and laity a way chosen by human nature, not imposed upon it by a wisdom that separates itself from human nature to rule it. But poetry does not escape the ineradicable fault of the wisdom-professions. It, too, presupposes a silent laity! The virtue poetry has of conceiving itself as the voice of the laity is lost in the professionalism of the voicing. (*The Telling*, 65)

This commitment to authority and power is a commitment to the illusions of truth. The illusoriness, for Riding, is signaled by the distance that poetry opens between itself and the "silent laity." That distance, frequently seen as (and called) "beauty," measures the failure of the project of truth to which language is ideally committed: for the revelation of truth through language occurs, so far as Riding is concerned, only as an interactive event. "The technique of poetry cannot be brought to a point of intensity at which the silent laity is *given* its universal speech" (*The Telling*, 66), for language is a social practice.

In her preface "To the Reader" of the 1938 *Collected Poems* Riding had raised this problem, but there she saw it not as a problem for poetry as such, only for poetry that had failed in its mission. When the "laity," or readers, are placed in a secondary relation to the poet, "the result is that readers become mere instruments on whom the poet plays his fine tunes ... instead of being equal companions in poetry" (*Collected Poems*, xxiv). In *The Telling*, however, Riding argues that the problem lies in the nature of poetry as such, which is only another specialized form of language.

This second problem with poetry is closely related to the first:

> Late in my own poetic professionalism I renounced the satisfaction of poetic success in words. *The Telling* is descended from that renunciation. I speak in it at the common risks of language, where failure stalks in every word. In speaking that is under poetry's protection, failure is scared away until all's said; small felicities of utterance magnify themselves into a persuasive appearance of truth. This success of art poets ennoble to a significance of virtue; in words throbbing with virtuosity's purposefulness they see a moral glow. . . . But only a problem of art is solved in poetry. Art, whose honesty must work through artifice, cannot avoid cheating truth. (*The Telling*, 66–67)

In poetry, Riding says, aesthetic successes are the illusions of truth; worse still, by these successes "failure is scared away." Riding turns from poetry to prose in order to reacquire the ground of the possibility of truth-telling, that is, "those common risks of language, where failure stalks in every word."

The "failure" of poetry, then, lies (paradoxically) in its aesthetic (formal and apparitional) pretensions to power and completeness. These are specifically *ideal* illusions rooted in the mistaken notion that the oneness of truth is something abstract and conceptual. On the contrary, for Riding truth is a "telling," an enactment. Her project—her famous commitment to what she called the "one story that tells all there is to tell" (*The Telling*, 176)—must not be seen as a conceptual project. Rather, it is the continuous execution of that story, which has an infinite number of (possible and actual) realizations.[8] *The Telling* is a project "kept in companionship." Hence,

> I testify that my story of there being essentially and ultimately but one story is my utter own. Let it not be equated with anything else! This would compromise its worth as an offering to that possibility

of companionship—to the prospect of my story of the one story's retaining, in that companionship, its meaning, my meaning, of its being a story of a one story we have all to tell. Whatever distance remains between the outreaching margins of readers' thoughts and mine, let it be true distance, distance between ourselves, in their thought as theirs and myself in my thoughts as mine. This being so, nothing is lost, I think, should our approaches seem to come to nought: fate, I think, is honorable with us in the true difficulties, allowing us rebeginnings where they halt us. (176–77)

This passage, and some of the others I have cited, should go some way toward eradicating the idea that the post-poetical Riding has been seeking a transcendental ground of truth. This (not uncommon) view arises from a mistaken reading of Riding's and her husband's work on the (variously titled) "Dictionary of Rational Meaning," which was first announced in 1942.[9] The dictionary is not seen by Riding as an archive setting forth the "true meanings" that correspond to various words. A dictionary of rational meanings need not also be a dictionary of transcendental meanings. As we have already seen, Riding is keenly aware of the "difficulties" and "distances" that inhabit the social practice we call language—even when language is being executed, as in *The Telling*, with utmost clarity and truth. Riding is certainly opposed to a language that opens a distance between a "laity" and the "wisdom-professions," but she is committed to a language that releases the "risks" of truth-telling— a language that is involved with what she called "true distance." This is a view of language as dialectical. Insofar as language performs its transmissive functions, it is a means not of sending but of exchanging messages.

Riding's distinction between true and false "distances" rests in her special view of language. Its "truth" does not depend upon an abstract correspondence between "words and things." Like mind, language for Riding should not be understood formally or structurally. Mind and language are activities. So, when she says of the dictionary that its

object is the demonstration of the dependence of good (in all the senses) diction on the use of words with attentive regard for their rational nature, and the general function of language as the articulation of our humanness (*The Telling*, 70) we do best to pay our own "attentive regard" to the wordplay operating in that parenthetical remark about "all the senses." An "attentive regard to [the] rational nature" of words means giving close attention to their "articulation" (which is always a *sensible* event, oral or scriptural, executed in social space). Riding does not use the word "diction" in some narrow and abstract way—indeed, she specifically equates it with the word "style."[10] For her, "good . . . diction" involves "all the senses"; and we are to note that she says "the senses" (rather than "its" senses) because that way of speaking reveals the eventual character of "diction": diction as an "articulation." It emphasizes as well the fact that human "rational nature" is embodied, material, and (ultimately) social and interactive.[a]

One of Riding's culminant poems, "When Love Becomes Words," argues the position she wishes to define. The poem maps the passage of "love" from an event of bodies to an event of words: "First come the omens, then the thing we mean" (p. 349). In love's more developed condition, "There are, in truth, no words left for the kiss" when love becomes words, for the words themselves enter upon the literal truth of human experience. In this new literalness

> love or utterance shall preserve us
> From that other literature
> We fast exerted to perpetuate
> The moral chatter of appearance.   (p. 350)

The prose point (as it were) of these lines is to show that all experience—whether it be "verbal" or "corporal"—is a kind of "literature"; or, as our twentieth-century idiom would have it, that language is the defining term of human experience. "When Love Becomes Words" does not involve the banishment of corporal experience:

> Think not that I am stern
> To banish now the kiss, ancient,
> Or how our hands or cheeks may brush
> When our thoughts have a love and a stir
> Short of writable and a grace
> Of not altogether verbal promptness.

[a] So when Joyce Wexler speaks of "Riding's long-held belief that the mind, not the senses, could apprehend ultimate reality" (146), she misunderstands Riding's view of "mind." Riding's ideas are much closer to those set forth in Mark Johnson's *The Body in the Mind: The Bodily Basis of Meaning, Imagination, and Reason* (Chicago: University of Chicago Press, 1987).

On the contrary, "finding ourselves not merely fluent/ But ligatured in the embracing words/ Is . . . still a cause of kiss among us,"

> Though kiss we do not—or so knowingly
> The taste is lost in the taste of the thought.

Kissing under the horizon of language is to enter the full reality of love—a love that knows itself as such. It is, in a wholly non-Lawrentian sense, to have brought about the realization of "sex in the head." In that state "we have ceased only to become—and are."

As Riding deploys her linguistic "metaphor of love" (p. 350) in this poem, "corporal" action is imaged in oral terms, whereas the action of thought is figured scripturally. This is a heuristic distinction only, for language is the universal (but non-transcendental) human condition. Nevertheless, Riding's work does tend to operate with this form of the distinction, as if she set a special privilege upon scripted language—as if oral language were too impermanent, like the body:

> And then to words again
> After—was it—a kiss or exclamation
> Between face and face too sudden to record.   (p. 351)

Riding's distinction between love written and love spoken, I think, anticipates her later distinction between poetry and prose. On one hand is "omen," on the other "meaning"; the one a thing of "becoming," the other of reality, of what we "are." However that may be, "When Love Becomes Words" illustrates very well Riding's ideas about language, reality, and that deepest form of human being, love.

When Riding turned to prose after 1938, the event had many anticipations in her poetry. In her wonderful prose poem "Poet: A Lying Word," for example: "Does it seem I ring, I sing, I rhyme, I poet-wit? Shame on me then" (*Collected Poems*, 237). To avoid this Riding constructs a prose poem that is a wall of words: "This wall reads 'Stop!' This poet verses 'Poet: a lying word!'" The poem presents two kinds of walls, a "false wall" that is associated with "the poet," and the "true wall" that is associated with the verbal text of the work before us. In "Poet: A Lying Word" Riding's text speaks itself:

> Stand against me then and stare well through me then.
> I am no poet as you have span by span leapt the high
> words to the next depth and season, the next season

> always, the last always, the next. I am a true wall:
> you may but stare me through.

Part of the strength of the poem lies in its prose formality, which serves as a clear visual trope for the "true wall" of language. That true wall, this text's language, speaks of finalities:

> And the tale is no more of the going: no more a
> poet's tale of a going false-like to a seeing. The
> tale is of a seeing true-like to a knowing.

The text is the "last barrier long shied of in your elliptic changes." As a thing that cannot be overleapt or gone beyond, it defines the ground of changing things. By its encounter "Comes this even I, even this not-I, this not lying season . . . this every-year." Finality comes in and as language; it *is* language. Language is the speaker of this text, speaking the permanent truth concealed in the particular, historically located utterances of the poet.

In a text like this we witness—as the title of a related poem puts it—a "Disclaimer of the Person." The ambiguous identity of the "I" is Riding's device for attempting a revelation of what is permanent and transpersonal in her own transient subjectivity.

> Past the half-way mark, historically, in my poems, and up to a last phase, I am much preoccupied to make personally explicit the identity of myself poet and myself one moved to try to speak with voiced consciousness of the linguistic and human unities of speaking: I am restive insofar as this [latter] identity is only an implicit principle in my poetic speaking.[11]

Riding here is speaking once again of the relation between her story and the one story. Whether one uses poetry or prose, our involvement with language necessarily divides "myself . . . and myself." In every particular deployment of language there is an "implicit principle" and presence of the transparticular ("the linguistic and human unities of speaking"). The operation of this "implicit principle" in language turns the (his)story of Riding's own poetical career into an episode in the tale of the truth. Her life as a poet displays

> a movement of developing sensibility, above the personal or professional, reflecting consciousness-at-large of the approach of human life in the whole to a term. (*Persea*, 416)

When Riding stops writing poetry, the event signals precisely "the approach of human life to a term." At that point there are no other walls to overleap. One stops seeking-after; one becomes absorbed into the process of seeking-after, into what she calls "human life in the whole." Language enters that life of its own which all human beings—the living as well as the dead—participate in.

My discussion of Riding's work has focused on those features which, in my view, bring at once challenge and opportunity to later writers. I shall conclude this part of the argument by looking at one final work by Riding, her outrageous satire "The Life of the Dead," which is the last work printed in the *Collected Poems*. I choose this text because it helps to summarize my discussion to this point.

"The Life of the Dead" explicitly represents itself as an effort to free Riding's English poetry from its poeticalness. In her prefatory "Explanation" of the text Riding discusses the origin and procedures of the work. It comprises ten sections of verse, each headed with an illustration executed by John Aldridge according to designs conceived by Riding. The sections contain a French text followed by its English equivalent, or translation. "The illustrations," Riding says, "are the germ of the text" and were conceived first, "as verbal comedies (!)." When the illustrations were worked out, "I then made the textual frames out of French—though French is not 'my' language." The French text serves as "the critical intermediary between the pictures and the English." Riding summarizes her object in this way:

> This highly artificial poem was first written in French, in order that the English might benefit from the limitations which French puts upon the poetic seriousness of words. (*Collected Poems*, 417)

The "critical intermediary" of the French text enables Riding to render what she calls a more "'literal' account of the world":

> The phrase 'poetic prose,' which is generally applied in a flattering sense to a degenerate form of prose-writing, may be correctly applied here because the poetic dishabille of the text is wilful, a conscious relaxation of poetic energy, not a stylistic orgy in prose. (*Collected Poems*, 417–18)

The illustrations, for their part, stand as textual equivalents for the poetry's desire to express "the real," which in this case is that simulacrum of reality Riding calls a period of modern life, and of modern art and literature especially, in which liveliness seemed moribund, and a lie of life was breathed into death, in the name of reality. ("Excerpts," *Persea*, 418)

A complex poetical procedure is being installed in order to satirize not merely the modern world (ca. 1933, when the work was published), but more pertinently the way that world imagines its own powers of expression and imagination. Once again we are delivered over to a text that is constructing an argument about language, poetry, and truth.

Riding's purpose is to tell the truth about the dead modern world and its dead poetry. To do this, she needs a linguistic equivalent in which the "moribund" truth will be revealed in a language that conveys "the whole truth" about this deadly subject. The device of "translation" pushes Riding's English text toward a stylistic level that appears (aesthetically) threadbare.

> Romanzel, doubtful if such abstruse goddess be
> Terrible to know, since only silence-mighty,
> Thinking amid the grim confusions
> Struggling ribbon-wise where seems her head
> To find a poetry of living death, resurrection
> Of all that dropped down false in life, impossible—
> Romanzel, spreading his tormented wings,
> Spreads the blank sky of the blank-eyed dead.
> Unidor, indifferent to the change
> From world to other world not seen,
> Holds the same task, contents the same desire.

This is grotesque and comical, a kind a cross between Charles M. Doughty's *The Dawn in Britain* and Rossetti's translations from the early Italian poets—both, for Riding, important moments for the understanding of modernism. The text's "poetic dishabille" stands as an index of the deceit that poetry's commitments to beauty always entail. The poem's debased style—artfully crafted—is the reflexive truth of its false appearances and public pretensions. Riding's text is trying to get hypocritical readers to face themselves and their false ideas about poetry, not least of all contemporary poetry.

Riding's flat "translated" style also opens a space between poetry's simulacra of beauty and the truth of those simulacra. The text preserves poetic apparitions in order that we should know them as such, in order

> To find a poetry of living death, resurrection
> Of all that dropped down false in life, impossible.

These lines, like the whole poem, are hypocritical, two-faced. By "prosing" the verse, Riding attacks the poetical resurrection of its living death. The arguments of *The Telling* are not far from this way of thinking about poetry. But the style of "The Life of the Dead" is very different because, in Riding's view, a properly executed prose does not lie open to the deceptions of verse.

In foregrounding its "highly artificial" character, "The Life of the Dead" puts Riding's textual "workshop" on display ("Excerpts," *Persea*, 418). One cannot read the poem without growing conscious of its composed features. Language-as-such rises up as the poem's central subject, therefore, and it rises up as a wall of joking and lying words. These words do not lead the reader anywhere, do not take the reader "false-like to a seeing." The poem is not allowed to point toward any truth beyond its own interactive features, its own textuality. The truth of the poem has become utterly literal. But in doing so it is not also set apart from the reader in some aesthetic condition of disinterest. The poem shows what its "textedness" assumes—that it carries within its own literality a reader's world of expectancies and exchanges. It is a wall of words "not to be scaled and left behind." "This wall reads 'Stop!' " and "'Stare me through.' " The argument is to avoid entering language (on the reader's or the writer's side) as if it were to be a "mortal simulacrum" of lying words pointing elsewhere (the deceptions of deep feeling, perhaps, or visionary transcendence of the immediate). We are not to be distracted from the literal drama of the text, as if its truth lay somewhere beyond the immediate communicative event.

A key feature of that drama is the poet's involvement in it. Riding's "workshop" is part of the work's "outrageous" comedy. The text disallows the illusion of a Shelleyan gap between "composition" and "inspiration." Insofar as a gap is opened in this text, then, it is opened between text and reader, with the latter encouraged to confront the text as utterly Other. In this way the reader is brought face to face with the word-as-such—with language as the entirety of the scene where truth as an exchange is represented. The writer (Riding) does not dominate (least of all "create") that scene, she inhabits it; in this sense language—the scene, its world, ourselves—speaks through her.

To sum up: Riding's work deals with three matters of special importance for later American writing. First, her turn toward prose signals the importance she attached to the rhetorical (as opposed to the symbolistic) features of language. Far from being asked simply to "overhear" the sublime reflections of the poet, the reader is forced to assume a position of active consciousness in face of her work. Second, her writing is a continuation of modernism's constructivist line (Pound, Williams, Stein, Oppen, Zukofsky) which emphasized the word-as-such. Third, Riding made a definitive swerve from romantic and "I-centered" poetry, along with all the ideological assumptions that came with that tradition (the most important of these is the idea of the poet as genius or creator). Engaging with these matters as she does, Riding brought the practice of poetry to a crisis. The example of her work stands as a vision of judgment for those who would follow. Her writing executes a standard of self-examination so deep and resolute that it cannot be decently evaded. Later writers who have not at least attempted to meet its challenge risk being seen—not least of all by themselves—as trivial, attendant lords and ladies.

"THE TRUE DIFFICULTIES, ALLOWING US REBEGINNINGS"   —Charles Olson

Laura Riding wrote a great deal of criticism and theoretical writing about writing. In this respect she stands in the modernist tradition and should be compared with Yeats, Pound, Stein, and Eliot. These kinds of polemical and philosophic commitments were largely foresworn by the next generation of poets. Spicer and Lowell are, it seems to me, philosophic poets, but neither would marshall the resources of prose (whether expository, polemical, or reflective) to pursue their intellectual and political commitments. The 1970s and 1980s, on the other hand, brought a distinctive return to such kinds of work in the experimental writing we have come to associate with Toronto, New York, and the Bay area.[b] In such contexts, procedural and stylistic ques-

[b] A vigorous scene of writing also orbits near Vancouver, B.C. It represents a conscious development of the work that came out of the other three centers. I should also mention the case (in England) of the poetry of Tom Raworth—recently discussed in *Critical Inquiry* by John Barrell ("Subject and Sentence: The Poetry of Tom Raworth," vol. 17 no. 2 [Winter 1991]: 386–409

tions of poetry began to be raised within the context of contemporary political and philosophic discussions.

Charles Bernstein, who stands at the center of so much contemporary experimentalism, has clearly accepted the terms in which Riding set the problem of poetry.[12] The question of language is central, as is the obligation to truth-telling and to a writing that decenters itself from the authoritative "I." Furthermore, the problem of poetry's relation to prose (and vice versa) is a recurrent preoccupation of Bernstein's work. *Content's Dream*, for example, is subheaded "Essays 1975–1984" but the collection itself calls into question the distinction between poetry and prose. "Three or Four Things I Know About Him" (which opens the collection); "A Particular Thing"; "G——": are these texts poetry or are they prose? It is not easy to say. Similarly, his books of "poetry" all print texts which do not, for various different reasons, "look like" poetry at all.

Bernstein's work signals a change that has come to the fore in American poetry during the past twenty years or so. The change appears whenever we see writers approaching their work through "the question of language" as it was initially framed by linguists like Saussure and philosophers like Wittgenstein. The work of Ron Silliman, in this respect, is exemplary. "It was Ed van Aelstyn," Silliman writes, "who, in his linguistics course, planted the idea (1968) that the definition of a language was also a definition of any poem: a vocabulary plus a set of rules through which to process it. What did I think poetry was before that?"[13]

This passage comes from Silliman's important "prose" piece "The Chinese Notebook." Its last question is telling. "The Chinese Notebook" is one of a large group of recent works—Genet's *Prisoner of Love* must be counted among them—where the borderline between imaginative and expository writing is called into question, or is lost, or is actively being shifted.[14] Silliman's text comprises a numbered set of reflections on various problems of writing and philosophy. An explicit parody of Wittgenstein's *Philosophical Investigations*, "The Chinese Notebook" raises the question of poetry's relation to truth both formally and substantively. The formal aspect of the problem is particularly crucial because (according to the received line of argument) poetry's failure as truth comes from its preoccupation with appearances. Is "The Chinese Notebook" philosophy or is it poetry? And if we say it is (or is not) one or the other, why and how do we arrive at our judgment?

156. What if I told you I did not really believe this to
be a poem? What if I told you I did?   (p. 59)

Because these are the kinds of problems "The Chinese Notebook"
keeps raising, the text offers itself as its own primary instance of the
issues it wants to address. The "question" of whether "The Chinese
Notebook" is expository (truth-telling) or poetic (a field of metaphoric nonidentities) appears as a question (literally) of style and
writing practice. The general question of poetry and truth arrives to
the reader in a particular and concrete form and—most importantly—*at the level of aesthetics*: What is the "truth" about the genre
of "The Chinese Notebook?" In Silliman's text, however, this question (it is one of many in the poem) cannot be answered (i.e., re-
sponded to) at an aesthetic level. It is not a hermeneutical but a
social, even a factual, question. It is also a "real" question in the sense
that it might be answered in various ways. "Interpreting the meaning" of the question(s) is not the only option in Silliman's poem. Or
perhaps we should say: "interpretation" and "meaning" may be pursued beyond the horizon of hermeneutics.

This kind of philosophical self-reflexiveness characterizes much
contemporary writing, especially contemporary experimental poetry.
The ethical and political question of poetry's truth therefore gets first
engaged as an epistemological self-interrogation. Poetry begins to
find its way back into the world by taking the world's question about
poetry seriously: what is its point, what is its truth? But it raises this
question as something that is relevant for anyone who uses language,
not just for poets (or critics). Metaphoric language will not disappear
simply because certain computer technicians want to develop noise-
free channels of communication. What can we mean by knowledge
if it is founded in language, and if language is foundationally a set of
differentials and nonidentities?

The epistemological problem of language must therefore be
faced—and not merely by the poets. By coming out of its aesthetic
tower, recent poetical writing—like the Lady of Shalott—has
shocked the well-fed wits of our modern Camelot—and not least
because in their descent from the tower the poets, like the lovely
lady, appear to have died to their office as poets. This "death of poetry" appears repeatedly as a technical and generic problem: is this
poetry, or what? Is it the Lady of Shalott or her dead remains? One
reads the work of Alan Davies (for instance, a piece like "Language

Mind Writing") or a critical text like Susan Howe's *My Emily Dickinson* only to experience a crisis of language. As in "The Chinese Notebook" and so many other recent texts, the dissolution appears as a problem of genre, a problem of what in the world (so to speak) poetry is. *My Emily Dickinson* looks like "literary criticism," and is catalogued as such by booksellers and libraries. It reads, however, like poetry—or seems constantly to draw its expository materials into poetical forms of expression, much as Emily Dickinson's letters are continually blurring the distinction between prose and poetry—frequently slipping altogether into ballad meter even as the physical text maintains the linear formalities of prose.[15]

Davies' text, originally delivered as one of the celebrated Langton Street "talks," observes the conventions of a certain kind of theoretical prose: Wittgenstein, Heidegger, perhaps Blanchot. But the text is so absorbed in its own expressiveness that reading it one may begin to lose track of the conventional distinction between words and things. The printed version of the text is divided into five sections that are as much poetical units ("stanzas") as they are rhetorical forms ("paragraphs"). The opening unit introduces the key ideas, but it does so by emphasizing their linguistic base. This happens through strategies of repetition, and in particular the repetition of key words/ideas—for instance, the words "Language," "Mind," and "Writing":

> Externalization is the detriment of language, of mind, of writing. There is something drastic in the magnitude of our thought of these things, and it is such that it does not permit them to separate except in thought, wherein they are entirely separate. It is mind that teaches us where we are wrong in writing. It is writing which teaches us wherein the languages are wrong, wherein a language is wrong. And it is language which, when an attentive tool, criticizes the obtrusive forms of the mind, and sharpens it, or them, making it that tool which separates all speech from thought, all speech from writing, and writing the arbiter of their graceful resubmissions. (*Signage*, 122)

The poetic elements here are the repetition patterns—of words, of sounds, of phrasings—whose presence is emphasized by the uniform flatness of the tonal field.

This textural artfulness presides over the work. Each of the three central paragraphs plays a series of exploratory games that spin around the three key words given in the title: paragraph two is executed under the sign "Language," paragraph three under the sign "Mind," and paragraph four under the sign "Writing." Finally, the fifth paragraph closes the piece by ringing various changes on the word "conclusion."ᶜ

The text does not cease to function as philosophic exposition. Nevertheless, its linguistic formalities—its sign structures—stand out in ways we associate with poetical rather than with philosophical works. As a consequence, textual apparitions and materialities begin to preoccupy our attention, as if the work's aesthetic features were the subject of the discussion—as if the text were an embodiment or enactment of thought, a demonstration (an example, a representation, a mimesis) of the idea that thought is always a certain kind of action—not a "truth" but, as Riding would say, a "truth-telling."

> Writing can't be an object because the world is a world of verbs and to write is a thing that someone does. Writing is an action in the world. Writing is the mind, any mind with language in its mind, and active in the world. (*Signage*, 132)

In a series of trenchant essays, some formal, some historical, Silliman has sketched a theory of what he has called "the new sentence."[16] The theory was partly developed in order to illuminate Silliman's writing practice (particularly in his ongoing work *The Alphabet*) as well as the work of some of his closest associates, like Kit Robinson and Barrett Watten. As a theory of the prose poem (or "poet's prose"),[17] however, its explanatory relevance extends well beyond its immediate objects. Davies, Susan Howe, Leslie Scalapino, and many others write "poet's prose," but the style of each is distinctive, and not at all like that of Silliman. Nevertheless, the procedures of "new sentence" writing, as sketched by Silliman, are useful for understanding all of this work.

In this context two matters carry special importance. First, such writing treats its formal and its semantic features as equally relevant to the logic of the text's development. Silliman's basic thought, for example, is that writing is thoroughly incarnate and eventual. As with Dante Gabriel Rossetti's poetry, a text's logical or cognitive elements are approached as physical units, and in this respect not to

ᶜThe text has other important and repeated words. In the opening paragraph, for example, the word "thought" is especially important, as are variations on the word "separate." The text foregrounds many words in this way.

be distinguished from the way we think of phonemes or morphemes. Silliman's texts attempt (as it were) to move the entirety of their action to the aesthetic or literal level. Second, the writing highlights its own procedural moves. The point here is to make the act of writing one of the principal subjects of the reader's awareness. As "the writer" thereby becomes a textual subject or function, the reader confronts the appearance of a text that is speaking itself.[18]

The notion that "Thought is Act" is Blakean. In the contemporary writing scene, where the conjunction of linguistics and philosophy localizes so many important issues of theory and writing, Blake's idea acquires a new suggestiveness for both poetry and philosophy. When thought is imagined as an event of language, "Text" replaces Blake's (Platonic) "Thought" as primary actant.

If the traditional quest of philosophy is to secure an identity of thought and its object, writers after Saussure and Wittgenstein can argue that poetry is now uniquely placed to explore that identification. For it is a commonplace of twentieth-century Western philosophy that we (can) only think in and through language (spoken or written). "Thought is Act," then, as it is "languaged"; and since language appears only as a material praxis, its very execution stands as the hitherto unsuspected model of the identity of thought and its (political) object. In contemporary writing, philosophical nominalism rises up to (re)assert a claim to truth and authority.

Such, at any rate, is the argument that is either implicit or explicit in many contemporary writers, both prose (the Oulipo group, for instance) and poetry (the so-called Language Writers in general). It is a (nominalist) argument based in a rejection of the idealist supposition that concepts or abstractions have an existence independent of the language in which they are framed, independent of the activity which generates those concepts and abstractions. When we read in Kathy Acker's recent *Empire of the Senseless* that "the demand for an adequate mode of expression is senseless," we have arrived squarely in the center of this tradition.[19] The aphorism locates "adequacy" of expression in an abstract region of "senseless" beings. For Acker, "expression" is a material and embodied event—not a matter of adequations but of extravagances and what Bataille calls a "general economy" of grace and expenditure. Those who seek after the "adequate mode of expression" operate in a restricted economy of supply and "demand," where people are moved senselessly (in both "senses") by abstract equations. In such a view, both neoplatonic and scientific models of thought are rejected because of their irreal aspirations toward establishing conceptual generalities for the orders of the world.[20]

The conjunction of theory with various kinds of imaginative writing in the 1970s and 1980s reflects, therefore, an important development for writers and philosophers alike. An "answer to Plato" is being formulated, and the answer is licensed by what I would have to describe as a nonmystical and nonromantic theory of poetry-as-inspiration. Paradoxically, Laura Riding is the immediate precursive exponent of such a theory. Riding turned away from poetry to prose in order to secure a language instrument that could tell the truth. In the contemporary scene, poetry is once again placed at the center of language by an argument that has constructed a theory and practice of "poetry" out of key elements of Riding's ideal of "prose." The argument grounds itself in an understanding of language as the practice of the forms of arbitrary signification. All aspects of language (or writing) are materialized (that is, they are approached through Jack Spicer's triad of morphemics, phonemics, and graphemics).[21] Indeed, author and audience are themselves exposed as functions of language, coded beings and sets of activities. When "poetry" is seen as the linguistic mode that calls attention to the activities of these codes, its truth-telling power appears in a new way. The physique and apparitions of poetry do not become, as they were for Riding, truth's obstacles and distractions. They become, rather, truth's own "tellings" and eventualities.

For human beings, to enter the world is to enter language—a world that is always-changing but ever-determinate and concrete, and a world no *one* ever made or could have made. It is a (social) world made by (and discovered as) language, through unceasing acts of textual intercourse. Their origin is not the God of Genesis creating ex nihilo and by an act of fission. The God of language was never alone or self-identical. This God therefore brings a new revelation to hi/story (which is our language). "Before Abraham was, I am": in the frame of reference I have been developing, this text is not the voice of Jesus, it is the voice of "Jesus" (and so the voice of God). It becomes a truth-telling statement (rather than a mere article of faith, or an absurd counterfactual) as soon as we understand that the text is "talking about itself." The text is, in this sense, an illustration of itself—at once report and example.

For Plato, the "problem with poetry" was its arbitrariness. Being inspired, the poets might and could say anything, and as Plato surveyed their various sayings he discovered much of what they said to be false (either false to fact, or false to accepted norms of virtue). He therefore dismissed them from the Republic until such time as they could justify their political presence.

After Plato certain lines of "defense" were raised for poetry. The first line, which descends from Aristotle, argues that poetry's (civic) function is to imitate reality, to create secondary worlds through which we can reflect upon—come to a better understanding of—the first orders of our lives. A second (neoplatonic) line of defense, made famous for English readers by Sidney's "Defence of Poesy," argues that poetry's office is to supply us with ideal models, golden worlds by which to transcend brazen circumstance.

A third line, which is perhaps a variant or extension of the second, emerged more recently as a critique of the inadequacies of poetry-as-mimesis. Blake's hostility to "Aristotles Analytics"[22] became, in the romantic view of poetry, a point of departure against the rationalisms of Aristotle and Plato: "I will not Reason & Compare: my business is to Create" (*Jerusalem*, 10:21). Romanticism replaced traditional reason with the generative "I" and the true voice of energetic feeling. In this view, poetry's partiality (in both senses) is acknowledged and even insisted upon. Human life is seen from a particular perspective, is seen as the possibility of many particular perspectives. Its "truth" consists in the completeness and honesty with which that perspective is presented and maintained. (The name for this perspective is "sincerity," and the office of the poet is to "teach . . . how" [*The Prelude*, XIV. 447] such a virtue may be acquired and practiced.)

The development of language theory in our century, exposed the arbitrary and conventional structure (the historicality) of Archimedean levers like reason, nature, imagination, sincerity. Philosophy continues to wrestle with the consequences of this exposure. The consequences for literature have been equally profound. "Theory" has gained a (bad?) eminence in literary criticism for its celebrated attacks upon "referentiality." Intertextual studies of various kinds have developed by avoiding the question of "reference," and hence by agreeing to confine the investigation of texts to studies of their formal and intersystemic features. Certain (theoretical) voices have consistently deplored not so much these practical studies as the philosophic grounds on which they are based. The critique is well-known:

"theory" turns literature into a mere game, a play of signifiers and signifieds. In this view, "theory" is an abandonment of the effort to find or establish the truth-functions of imaginative writing.

In the practice of the poets, however, "theory" has had very different—profoundly different—consequences. This has come about because the poets' interests in theory and language are not the same as the interests of the philosophers and the literary academics. The latter have engaged their "wars of theory" in an effort to defend certain conceptual/ideological positions (by acts of promotion and acts of resistance). They are engaged in a struggle over practical ideas. When the poets make their resort to linguistics and philosophy of language, the issues at stake are the forms and transforms of language. For the poets, language is not something to be understood, it is something to be carried out.

In this sense, one will not "measure" the truth of thought (or language) by invoking a set of fixed standards. As Blake observed, bringing out number, weight, and measure merely signals a condition of dearth. If, however, "truth" is seen as a function of language—of thought as act—then the "measure of thought" becomes rhetorical and stylistic: "measure" in the poetical sense of the word. Charles Bernstein's important essay "Thought's Measure" argues such a view of thought and explores some of its implications for the practice of writing.[23]

Philosophically speaking, one cannot "comprehend" language because there are no extralinguistic positions from which it can be viewed. This view of language has induced a certain skeptical irony, or diminished pragmaticism, among many twentieth-century philosophers, as we know. For the poets, however, the understanding has come as a great opportunity to reimagine the relation of poetry to truth—ultimately, to reimagine the relation of thought to act. Plato's realm of Ideas is transvalued. "If it were writing we would have to explain" (*My Life*, 30): the tenth section of Lyn Hejinian's *My Life* begins with a move arguing—illustrating, really—that (this) poetry is not "writing" but performative text—what Spicer earlier called "Thing Language." Text (in this sense) does not have to be explained since no gap appears between thought and act, intention and execution. All the gaps are literal.

> It was awhile before I understood what had come between the stars, to form the constellations. They were at a restaurant owned by

Danes. Now that I was "old enough to make my own decisions," I dressed like everybody else. People must flatter their own eyes with their pathetic lives. The things I was saying followed logically the things that I had said before, yet they bore no relation to what I was thinking and feeling. There was once a crooked man, who rode a crooked mile—thereafter he wrote in a crooked style characteristic of 19th-century prose, a prose of science and cumulative sentences. (*My Life*, 36)

This kind of text is trying to be equal only to itself. As such, it extends Riding's quest for "love as love, death as death."[24] Whether a text proceeds "logically" or dissociatively, it is language with its whole world in its hands. Ideas, facts, identities: all are part of what language creates and executes.

In this imagination of language, our most ancient theory of poetry—that it is inspired discourse—begins to achieve a new persuasiveness. For when we decide that language comprehends reality (both being homologous sets of all possible apparitions), we simultaneously take it to be self-authorizing. Poetry's special privilege emerges at exactly this point, for poetry is that form of discourse whose only object is to allow language to display itself, to show how it lives. What was once named "God"—that Being whose center is everywhere and whose circumference is nowhere—has died and been reborn as language. So far as the poets are concerned, the linguistic apparition of God overgoes those two famous earlier transformations (the God of reason and philosophy, the God of nature and science). If language is ultimate reality, then only those in and through whom language reveals itself will be reliable sources of the truth of language, and hence of the reality of the world. Language is the common resource of our humanness, and in this sense—as both Wordsworth and Wittgenstein suggested—we are all privileged through language. But language, as Wordsworth also argued, has its seers. These are the poets (not the scientists/linguists or the literary critics/philosophers) because only the poets put language-as-such into play. The poets do not seek after that impossibility, the understanding of God (or a Godlike knowledge). Rather, they seek what Bernstein has named "The Simply"[25]: God's revelation (which is equally God's action in the world). In this sense, poetry is literally a Divine Action, for poetry is language practicing itself. In poetry, language lives and moves and has its Being.

CONTEMPORARY WRITING AND THE PRACTICE OF TRUTH

The consequences of this (poetical) way of transacting language are profound. I do not mean the conceptual consequences, which I have been sketching to this point, but the practical results traced out in recent poetry.

Consider, for example, this short poem by David Bromige:

> *The Point*
> The point is not the point—
> the hand that indicates,
> attended to, is meaningless,
> too familiar to engage—
>
> the barn that's indicated
> burns but what of that?
> We know wood catches fire.
> It's just sensational.
>
> Someone is pointing at the flames—
> attention has been caught,
> desire ignites—we see ourselves
> as someone points them out.

Like many of Bromige's poems, "The Point" adopts some familiar lyric conventions. Most important is the first-person voice that controls the ordering of the details. Bromige's poem is stylistically more self-conscious than most romantic lyrics, where the conventions of sincerity (the illusion of spontaneity) can never be altogether neglected. "The Point" is a brainy work. But it is also not abstract. It has a clear subject (poetry and the way it executes "meaning"), and it explores that subject by "taking itself for its text" (as it were). Not simply the allegorical scene constructed in "The Point," but even more crucially *the textual construction of that scene*, are the work's illustrative materials. The final stanza, for all its play of wit, could hardly be more explicit. Poetry, we observe, is not being directed toward (describable or referential) meaning, it is enacting a play of desire. The poetic text therefore appears as a dynamic of self-attention that reader and writer each transact.

The transaction is cooperative, even dialogical, as many of Bromige's poems show:

> *Untitled*
> > *for Merleau-Ponty*
>
> As I asked
> What is going to become
> of us, one fact
>
> escaped me, you
> were listening for me
> to complete a meaning,
>
> and looking at me
> was the fact I overlooked,
> looking at you.

This forthright text recalls nothing so much as a traditional dramatic monologue in an act of self-address. It is properly "Untitled" because it has no subject other than itself.

Poems like these—as the reference to Merleau-Ponty indicates—are fully conscious of "the linguistic turn" taken by philosophy in the twentieth century; indeed, they explicitly address topics that arise from the languaging of philosophy. The poems are, for all that, fairly traditional from a stylistic point of view. Bromige's work can be different—for instance, in the poem "If Wants to Be the Same":

> The mounting excitement
> as we move
> step by step
> of difference
> off the same
>
> *if* wants to be the same
>
> the same as *is*

Subject matter here is not far removed from "The Point" and "Untitled." But in this case the differential between *verbum* and *res* has been sharply reduced because the text employs so few "referential" markers. No figure of a writing poet hovers here (as it does in "Untitled"); the words "point" toward no (imaginary) "burning" buildings. The "we" speaks for (connects to) the words of this text itself. More elemental still, this "we" seems the speech of the letters, and especially certain key letters in this text (i, f, and s). To read this poem is to negotiate the excited play of language's differential transformations.[d]

I make one further comment on this poem. Language here is troped into an economy of desire, which the text associates with a particular form of language: poetry, or language in its "as if" mode ("*if* wants"). Language functions in many ways, and poetry has always been associated with the language of desire. When Bromige's poem recuperates that ancient tradition, however, desire is trans-(not de-) personalized. Individual desire finds its norm in a social rather than a psychological dynamic. In this sense the poem "expresses" not the language of desire but the desire of language. The difference is important, as one can see immediately from the opening line of Bromige's "Some (More) Dicta of William Blake": "The authors are in the alphabet." Bromige is parodying Blake's famous statement about his late epic works ("the Authors are in Eternity").[26] In each case poetry is represented as inspired discourse, but Bromige transforms Blake's idealist vocabulary to expose what he takes to be its primary truth: that all gods reside in the human breast, and hence that "inspiration" is incarnate, finite, historical. "The alphabet is happy to compose the book of love."

Once the authority for poetry is located in "the alphabet" rather than in the alphabet's infinite secondary constructions (specific historical selvings, materialities, and worlds), poetry's stylistic opportunities are dramatically increased. The astonishing inventiveness of early modernist writing marks the first phase of poetry's own "linguistic turn" in this century. The second came later, especially during the past twenty years, when certain (principally American) writers returned to modernism's constructivist traditions. Bromige's work is part of that second phase. His age, however (he was born in 1933), his long connection with the academy (he is a tenured professor at Sonoma State University), and perhaps his national origins (British), distinguish him from many of the writers he might otherwise be compared to because of shared philosophical and intellectual interests. His work appears much more traditional, for instance, than what we see in the following pair of texts (the opening passages of two poems by Bernstein, "I and the" and "The Klupzy Girl"):

[d]A poem like this encourages interpretational games. For example, one wants to suggest that the text's "we is a first person plural corresponding to the pair of first person singulars concealed in the two key words "if" and "is." This interpretation is (and should be), like language itself, an arbitrary creation which justifies itself only in the event (i.e., how far can we take such a train of thought?). From a philosophic point of view, such a correspondence clearly goes straight to the heart of the ancient question of the relation of poetry to truth.

I and the
to that you
it of a

know was uh
in but is
this me about
        *   *   *

The Klupzy Girl
Poetry is like a swoon, with this difference:
it brings you to your senses. Yet his
parables are not singular. The smoke from
the boat causes the men to joke. Not
gymnastic: pyrotechnic. The continuousness
of a smile—wry, perfume scented. Not this
would go fruity with all these changes
around. Sense of variety: panic. Like
my eye takes over from the front
yard, three pace. Idle gaze—years
right down the window. Not clairvoyance,
predictions, deciphering—enacting. Analytically,
i.e., thoughtlessly.

Texts like these violate basic traditional reading expectations. Not only can they appear to "make no sense," they may elicit strong hostility (especially from academic and "professional" readers) because they are evidently constructed with great deliberateness—as if the object were to be as "difficult" as possible.

There is no question that such texts mean to provoke the reader's attention, and particularly an attention to language and the word-as-such. This happens because of various textual deviances (from standard grammar within sentences, coherent style or idiolect, orderly rhetorical progression of sentences, etc.). Furthermore, as "poetry" they seem peculiarly indifferent to the rules of pleasure and beauty as these were (re)defined for poetry in the Kantian tradition. (The passages, in particular the second, recall Riding's quest for a "poetic dishabille of the text.")

At an elementary level such writing is designed to execute a cleansing of the doors of perception. These texts assume (a) that language as such is supremely important; (b) that traditional language use, and especially traditional poetry, often obscures language by wrapping it in what the romantics called "veils of familiarity"; and (c) that readers must be both independent and active agents in the scene of writing. Truth-telling is imagined in both passages as the practice of conscious thought (in both writer and reader) with respect to language. What is *not* imagined is the assumption that the reader's part in poetry is to decipher and translate "meaning(s)" that might be presumed to lie behind sets of authored words. Because everything in these texts is pushed to an extreme literalness, the traditional herme-neutic structure of reading is tilted slightly and put out of order. The reader is not being asked to explicate what the passages "mean" be-cause the texts are not being controlled by a traditional medium/ message structure.

None of this is to say that these texts are meaningless. On the contrary, they have been constructed exactly to generate thought and ultimately "meaning." The reader's activity is called forth, but not in order to supply the text with a meaning which it shrinks from clearly disclosing. The reader's activity is called out in order to make it part of the textual field, in order to have reading exposed for what it is: an assumed textual presence. Reading does not come "after" the text, as a "response"; reading is the correspondence which writing has al-ready foretold.

In the first text, for instance, we are informed (in a note to the poem) that it was "compiled from *Word Frequencies in Spoken Ameri-can English* by Hartvig Dahl." Dahl's work "was based on transcripts of 225 psychoanalytic sessions involving 29 generally middle-class speakers averaging in age in the late twenties." "I and The" is con-structed from the "17,871 different words" used by these speakers; the poem is twenty-two pages long and presents its words (as the passage shows) three to a line, in "stanzas" of three lines, with the words arranged "in descending order" of their frequency of use (*Sophist*, 8on.).

"I and The" is thus a kind of "found text"—that is its chief generic convention. By arranging the words in arbitrary triads, however, Bernstein makes a gesture of active intervention. His (prose) note to the text, which is part of his intervention, suggests that these words express a kind of political or social unconscious for a certain class of (contemporary) Americans. Bernstein's interventions throw an arbi-trary set of organizing forms over the words. The presence of these forms has a profound effect on the words, which are opened toward the possibility of multiple relationships and meanings. Particular meanings and relationships are left to the imagination of the reader (for instance, when I read this text I hear in the opening line an "allusion" to Martin Buber's classic *I and Thou*). As we proliferate these kinds of meaning we are brought to assent implicitly to one of this work's most important arguments: that language as such has a fate of meaning. It is as if one were able to glimpse in language an enduring human presence, as if the "one story" of that presence were unable *not* to reveal itself, no matter how atomized, unconscious, and fractured that presence appears to be. Not only do we hear poems inhabited by voices, we discover that our own voices appear to have awaited our arrival.

The other text (the opening lines of "The Klupzy Girl") works somewhat differently, and it illustrates a different feature of this kind of writing. Once again we observe an arbitrary arrangement of linguistic forms only this time it is the sentence (rather than the word) which is taken as the principal unit of construction. These sentences do not proceed by any of the rhetorical, narrative, or psychological orders that are customary in poetry. The arrangement, as in "I and The," is stochastic.

Though "difficult" in certain respects, the poem is structurally quite simple: a theme is stated in the opening sentence, and the text that follows elaborates the theme. But the elaboration is carried out as in action painting, or in music, for in this text there are no ideas but in things—and here the "things" are all verbal. The passage is a "pyrotechnic" display—a literal "enacting"—of what the first sentence names "difference." The poem is an effort to restore thinking to its senses (in both senses) through an elaborate play of metaphors that are forced to operate simultaneously at literal and cognitive levels.

The poem, it should be observed, does not deny the "panic" that comes with the dissociative "Sense of variety" encouraged by "all these changes/ around." Panic and dissociation are permanent features of "the one story" and its whole truth, the inverses of our particular (vain) efforts to capture the story in a definitive form. The text works continually to sweep us off our feet, to undermine that (literally, counterproductive) rage for order and meaning which this passage alludes to in its last sentence: "Analytically/ i.e., thoughtlessly."

Analytics and finality are also part of the story—the part where thoughtlessness comes into play. Analysis brings the "changes" (and along with them, thinking) to a halt. Analysis brings us from "thinking" (or "telling") to thoughts and ideas. The halt has to be temporary, however, because all parts of this process are grounded in language, which is a human activity in a state of perpetual change.

Laura Riding grew wary of poetry because its "verbal rituals . . . court sensuosity as if it were the judge of truth" (*Persea*, 414). The linguistic splendor of much contemporary writing—for example, the passages from Hejinian and Bernstein, quoted above—might easily be taken as an example of just what Riding most objects to in poetry. Hejinian and Bernstein could no doubt reply, out of Riding's own work, that truth is brought to judgment through language; that language is inherently sensuous and material; and—most important— that the truth expressed through language is most fully rendered in poetry, which is the one form of language committed to full self-disclosure. Poetry is "the telling" of the whole truth; it is at the same time "the judge" (however mortal) of its truth-telling because it makes its own actions a main subject of attention and judgment.

In such a view—it is widespread in the contemporary scene— poets have more to say, and more ways to say it, exactly because they think of their work in relation to (the philosophy of) language rather than (the philosophy of) imagination. The "texts" appear to say more than the writers could have imagined for themselves. "The self is unravelled as an example in investigating particular historical events, which are potentially infinite."[27] Speaking through them rather than being made to speak for them, language multiplies poetry's stylistic opportunities. The best writers of the past twenty years, therefore, have succeeded just because they agreed to enter the prison house of language. It is, of course, where we all live, but only those who inhabit it deliberately are able to tell the truth about it.

4

The Poetry of Truth. A Dialogue (on Dialogue)

GILBERT: Dialogue . . . can never lose for the thinker its attraction as a mode of expression. By its means he can both reveal and conceal himself. . . .

ERNEST: By its means, too, he can invent an imaginary antagonist, and convert him when he chooses by some absurdly sophistical argument.

GILBERT: Ah! it is so easy to convert others. It is so difficult to convert oneself. To arrive at what one really believes, one must speak through lips different from one's own. To know the truth one must imagine myriads of falsehoods.

—OSCAR WILDE, "The Critic as Artist. A Dialogue. Part II"

That mask! That mask! I would give one of my fingers to have thought of that mask.

—DENIS DIDEROT, *Rameau's Nephew*

[Interlocutors: Georg Mannejc, Anne Mack, J. J. Rome, Joanne McGrem, Jerome McGann]

GM. And so we will find it possible to get beyond the magical idea of knowledge—the idea of knowledge as control and mastery, the *ideal* of that idea. Instead we shall have this display and celebration of our differences.[a]

AM. Our differences about what?

[a]Mannejc here approaches dialogue from a distinctly Heideggerian point of view—the same that dominates,

GM.   About anything! This talk of ours, these conversations, what are they grounded in? Not the pursuit of truth (that old ideal of philosophy and science), not the pursuit of power (that old ideal of magic and technology). They are grounded in the pursuit of meaning, the desires of interpretation. And interpretation proceeds according to a dialogical rather than a systems-theoretical or systems-correcting model. Dialogues are governed by rules of generosity and ornamentation, not rigor and method.

AM.   Ah, the adorable dialogical imagination! How the star of Bakhtin has risen in the West—and who am I to challenge its ascendancy?

But what are you saying, exactly? Is this to be an unrestricted play of interpretation? Does anything go? Will all the Lord's people be queuing up for haruspicators' licenses?

GM.   That's cheap—you've been reading too much Hilton Kramer. Our most sophisticated traditions of interpretation call for nothing less than the reader's complete freedom. In Hebrew midrash, as we know, reading is "divergent rather than convergent . . . moving rather than fixed . . . always opening onto new ground . . . always calling for interpretation to be opened up anew." Many still "understand the conflict of interpretation as a deficit of interpretation itself, part of the logical weakness of hermeneutics." This "prompts the desire to get 'beyond interpretation' to the meaning itself. . . . [But] my thought is that this very [desire] implies a transcendental outlook that has, in Western culture, never been able to accept the finite, situated, dialogical, indeed political character of human understanding, and which even now finds midrash to be irrational and wild."[1]

The need to possess the truth, the fear of doubt and uncertainty. It is the fear from which Arnold fled, in the middle of the nineteenth century—the fear of a democratic conversation moving without benefit of authoritative touchstones. Arnold saw it as the spectrous dialogue of the mind with itself. And he had reason to fear that dialogue, which can be unnerving or even worse. It can overthrow altogether what one takes to be the truth: the soul of the world's culture

for example, the anthology recently put together by Tullio Maranhao, *The Interpretation of Dialogue* (Chicago: University of Chicago Press, 1990). But because Mannejc represents this point of view in a dialogical (rather than an expository or a narrativized) form, his position opens itself to critique and disconfirmation. The form of the dialogue puts "the interpretation of dialogue" into question. It urges us to see *scientia* not as states of knowledge but as practices of knowing.

Of course, hermeneutics traditionally frames its own pursuit of knowledge in similar terms. The point is that its traditional methods, which are serial and expository, limit its critical powers. Concepts form part of a specific social practice; they comprise the ideological horizon of their practice. What is crucial to dialogue—as the form is represented in the present case—is that it calls critical

suddenly brought face to face with the mask of the god's anarchy—and a mask appearing, in its most demonic guise, as a polished surface reflecting back the image of one's self, the *hypocrite lecteur* loosed upon the occidental world in Arnold's day by Baudelaire.

JJR. [speaking to GM] You call this a "celebration" of differences, but to me it seems more a clash, and thus a struggle toward that truth you are so ready to dispense with. Dialogue is less a carnival than a critical exchange in which the errors and limits of different ideas are exposed to conflict.

It is all very well to float above this struggle, observing it as a rich display of energy, a celebration of itself. Thus we become the romantic inheritors of the deities of Lucretius.

> I sit as God holding no form of creed,
>   But contemplating all.
>
>   (Tennyson, "The Palace of Art," 21–12)

But in the world where our talk goes on, we are not gods; we are, as you suggested, political animals. Your ivory tower of interpretation is a particular political position, and the fact is that I don't agree with it. Unlike yourself, I believe these conversations *are* grounded in the pursuit of truth, and *do* involve the struggle of power.

GM. I'm not interested in the contemplative life. Dialogue involves various persons and is, as I say, necessarily political. What I mean to "celebrate"—and I don't apologize for it—is the power of dialogue to harness ideas, to generate new and interesting forms of thought.

JJR. But you don't seem inclined to make the necessary distinctions or discriminations. Some "forms of thought" are more interesting than others, some are trivial, some are not. What's important about dialogue is that it helps to expose those distinctions, to sort them out. For instance, I wouldn't say that your ideas about dialogue are trivial or uninteresting; but I would say they are wrong. There's a difference between us. Would *you* say I was wrong in these ideas—are you prepared to argue that I'm wrong in my judgments about your judgments?

attention to its own conceptual commitments in ways that traditional interpretive forms do not. In this sense, we do not interpret dialogue, it interprets us (with "us" standing here equally for those who speak and for those who listen)—and it does so exactly to the extent that we answer its call to participate in its exchanges.

Mannejc's position, therefore, seems to me slightly alienated from itself. We should read it not simply as an exposition of certain ideas, but as the drama of their exposition. The difference is small but finally crucial. Here, I think, we do not really get an "interpretation of dialogue" but "dialogue as interpretation."

GM. Yes, you are wrong.

JJR. Why, how? On your showing, how *could* I be wrong?

GM. Because what I was saying has nothing to do with being right or being wrong. That's another matter entirely.

JJR. Another "language game"?

GM. Perhaps—why not?

JJR. Because under those conditions, as I said before, "anything goes." Shift the language game and what was "wrong" becomes something else—it becomes, perhaps, "interesting" or "uninteresting," or perhaps even "right."

Don't misunderstand me. I am as aware as you are that context alters the status and even the meaning of what we see and what we think. The "pursuit of truth" is toward an imaginable (as opposed to an achievable) goal. We have to be satisfied with what we *can* acquire—knowledge, the historical form of truth. Nevertheless, that goal, "the truth," *must be imagined* if certain kinds of intellectual activities can be pursued.

AM. Truth as a necessary fiction? You're as unscrupulous and manipulative as Georg. "Knowledge, the historical form of truth": come off it! Does the "truth" you want to "imagine" exist in the same order as the "knowledge" you say we can gain? If it doesn't, how do we get it?

JJR. We don't "get" it, as if by a process of discovery.

AM. Maybe we get it like a disease?

GM. Truth as a disease! What an interesting idea.

JJR. Be serious. We construct the truth, we imagine it. Or do you imagine that the work of imagination is somehow less real—less human and historical—than the work of knowledge?

And what about *your* metaphor: "necessary fiction!" The implication being, apparently, that what we imagine is somehow less substantial than what we labor to discover and construct. How did Keats put it? "What the imagination seizes as Beauty must be Truth—whether it existed before or not."[2] Created work, whether primary—like the material universe—or secondary—like history itself, or Plato's dialogues, or the Bible: these are not *fictions* in the sense you seem to suggest. They are original forms of Being—and in the case of secondary creations like poetry, original forms of Human Being. Knowledge—science—is not their source, could not bring them into existence. Rather, knowledge takes these things (as well as itself) for its subject.[b]

And this is why I stand with Plato and Socrates on the matter of dialogue and conversation. Dialogue is how we pursue the truth through the clash of different views. It is our oldest tool for testing—and correcting—the limits of our thinking.

AM. But there are "intellectual activities" where "the truth" will not be, must not be, "imagined."

JJR. You mean, I suppose, scientific or technological activities.

AM. No I don't. I had in mind Plato's dialogues, the Bible: creative and poetical work in general.

JJR. Well, if you wanted to surprise me, you've succeeded. I would have thought it obvious that these are the very and perhaps even the *only* works where "the truth" *will and must be* "imagined."

AM. You're so obsessed with the idea of "the truth" that you impoverish your own imagination. And so you misunderstand me—as usual.

I wasn't suggesting a distinction between poetry and imagination, but between imagination and truth. And by that distinction I was asking you to rethink the way imagination acts in a poetical field. What the imagination seizes as beauty is not, cannot, and must not be "truth." Rather, it seizes appearances, phenomena, *facticities*. The physique of the poetical event: from the elementary phonic values of the letters and syllables, through the entire array of verbal imagery, to the shape of the scripts and all the physical media—material as well as social—through which poetry is realized. What the imagination seizes as beauty is not truth, it is the image of a world. The question of truth may and will be brought to bear on that world, as it is always brought to bear on our larger world; but that question is

[b]Rome here alludes to Anne Mack's ideas about "hypothetical histories" which she proposed in a different conversation. I quote from her remarks:

"If Literary History is to be written . . . it must create a textual environment in which poems and poetry can be reborn into new worlds. Like Keats's Ruth, the poems must be 'stood in tears amidst the alien corn.' That is what a literary antihistory might do. The poems must stand as if they were alive, but also as if they stood in a world elsewhere, alienated from any original home. Literary History, like the poems themselves, will then tell us equally of origin and of alienation, and of the relations that these two conditions (or moments) keep with each other. . . .

"One starts by imagining an impossible object— let us call it 'the origins of English romanticism.' Every historian knows that even the simplest event

not brought to bear in or by the poetry itself. God does not put questions of truth to his creations, and neither do poets. As Blake's prophet of the poetical, Los, says: "I will not Reason & Compare: my business is to Create" (*Jerusalem*, 10:21).

JJR. Perhaps divine creation may be imagined as a seizure of pure beauty.

GM. Does that make "beauty" a kind of disease?

AM. Shut up, Georg. [to JJR] I'm sorry I set him off. Go on with what you were saying.

JJR. Well, if divine creation might be imagined a perfect form of beauty, human creations are nothing of the sort. Poetry, for instance, being a form of language, comes to us (as one is meshed in a network of incredibly complex relations which no one could hope to unravel. So the quest for 'the origins of English romanticism' is an imaginative and hypothetical journey from the start—it is anti-historical, a romance quest, anti-history.

"In that case, why even bother, one might ask? And the answer is that the quest is undertaken not to discover 'the origins of English romanticism,' but to clarify the various ways this imaginary object might be defined and interpreted. For example, to re-imagine 'the origins of English romanticism' through a recovery of *The Florence Miscellany* and Della Cruscan poetry in general is to suggest a whole new series of related reimaginings. And so the ultimate object of the immediate hypothetical project emerges. We would not only have to read and re-evaluate a considerable body of unfamiliar poetry and cultural materials, we would have to re-read and re-evaluate the cultural deposits that have grown so familiar to us—perhaps, indeed, all too familiar. And we would have to re-read and re-imagine the instruments by which our received books of memory and forgetting were made.

"I am not simply calling for a more compendious and encyclopaedic history—something like the fifteen-volume Cambridge History of English Literature, where we are given the materials to see (for example) 'the origins of English romanticism' in a variety of possible perspectives. The Cambridge History's encyclopaedic character —its mass of details and scholarly apparatus—undermine the work's inertia toward coherent explanatory narrative. It is history and anti-history at the same time. But its anti-historical potential is too obedient to the (historian's) signs of accuracy and thoroughness.

"What I have in mind is a history at once more energetic and imaginative—a history that assumes the past has not yet happened, that it remains to be seen. If a history is to reflect its subject back to us, then the ideal literary history will be a structure of hypothetical worlds.

"These will have to be very precisely formulated. To stay with our possible topic 'the origins of English romanticism,' I imagine a critical narrative unwinding from suppositions like this: If we suppose romanticism to be structured on the double helix of the naive and the sentimental, what is the historical place, in English romanticism, of Burns's *Poems, Chiefly in the Scottish Dialect* (1786)? Or of Sir William Jones's translations of the Vedic hymns published in the mid-1780s? Or of the Della Cruscans' poetry, Blake's *Songs*, or the *Lyrical Ballads*?

"Then one might advance other suppositions altogether. The best history of this kind, to plagiarize Byron, will 'suppose this supposition' itself, exposing the hypothetical character of the historical constructions and thereby encouraging other hypotheses. This kind of history builds upon suppositions that are concretely realized possibilities, upon imaginations that already have their names and habitations. The point is to reveal what has already taken place as something that might be imagined, and to explain why we carry out this imagining. Shelley said it exactly: 'We must imagine what we know.' To do so is to reveal, not the truth of fact or of reason, but the truth of imagination as it operates in history" (from "What is the History of Literature. A Dialogue in Two Fyttes," unpublished).

might say) "legend laden"ᶜ with the conflicts of truth and error, good and evil. Whatever one thinks of primary worlds, all secondary ones are ideological.

ʿJJR's thinking seems haunted by Keats. This phrase is from "The Fall of Hyperion," Canto II, line 6.

GM.   Just so. And interpretation is the way we engage these kinds of acts. Science and philosophy are other kinds of acts altogether.

AM.   [speaking to GM] What nonsense. Poetry, Interpretation, Science, Philosophy: these are medieval distinctions and they'll get us nowhere.

Besides, there is a difference, even on your showing, between poetry and its interpretation—between, for instance, the bible and its commentators. Or don't you think so? Is there not an inspired text—the poem—that is different from the reading of that text—the interpretation?

GM.   Of course, but it isn't a difference whose "truth" we can ever be clear about. Because it's a difference always being defined ex post facto, that is, under the sign of its interpretation. The bible itself—every poem we engage with—already comes to us under hermeneutical signs. "When composition begins, inspiration is already on the decline": Shelley's famous remark involves a profound understanding of the nature of texts.³ If we ask of the Bible, for example, "where in this work can the Word of God be found," we will not get a clear answer. Because the concept of location is a secondary and interpretive concept. When skeptics debunk the bible's pretension to be "the Word of God" by pointing out the endless diaspora of its texts, their insight—though not their conclusion—is acute. The Word of God is a circle whose center is everywhere and whose circumference is nowhere.

The same must be said of all imaginative works—of every work that comes before us under the sign of creation. The bible is merely the masterwork of all those works—the originary revelation of "the eternal act of creation in the infinite I Am."⁴

JJR.   If that is so, then ideology—good and evil, truth and error—must be involved in that eternal act of primary creation. Which makes perfect sense since—as Blake saw so clearly—god and the gods are creatures of Man's imagination.⁵ Stories to the contrary—like the story in Genesis—are just exactly that—stories to the contrary.

But I digress into theology and maybe even deconstruction, and neither discipline interests me very much. What does interest me is another, related implication I see in your remarks. I put it as a question: What is the status of error, evil, failure in poetical work? Like yourself, most are happy to imagine the carnival of interpretation, the dialogue of endless errant reading. But if the primary texts are themselves errant and ideological, how are we to read them? Certainly not as transcendent models. They seem, in this view, more like images of ourselves: confused, mistaken, wrong—and perhaps most so when we imagine them (or ourselves) reasonably clear and correct. If poetry delivers the best that has been known and thought in the world, it falls sadly short of our desires.

GM.   Perhaps what Arnold meant was that it gave us the best of all possible worlds—where the possibilities are understood, from the start, as finite and limited. That, in any case, seems to be Shelley's point in his remarks about composition and inspiration.

JJR.   And perhaps the optimal of this possibility comes not from poetry's "perfection" so much as from the completeness of its self-presentation? Then the shortfall of desire would arrive without the illusion that it could have been otherwise. And it would arrive that way because the message and the messenger—the poems themselves—are implicated in that shortfall of desire. So we come to Shelley once again: when composition begins, inspiration is already on the wane—you know the rest.

GM.   Ah yes, the mind in creation is as a failing code.

AM.   [ignoring GM's last remark] But suppose, as Jay said earlier, that the poems *are* "errant and ideological"—just like the interpretations of the poems? Shelley was never happy about the didactic aspects of his own work, even though he—quite rightly too—couldn't abandon his didacticism. His theory of inspiration waning through composition seems to me part of the long-playing record he left us of his uneasiness on this score.

Most professors tend to read his theory in a Kantian light—by which I mean they hold out an ideal of poetry that transcends ideology and didacticism. Look at the way Browning is read, for instance. His dramatic monologues, we are told, escape the didactic subjectivism of Browning's early romantic mentor. So a poem like "My Last Duchess" becomes a model of poetic objectivity.

GM.   Quite rightly too. For in Browning's dramatic monologues the romantic lyric is "dramatically replayed" and historicized. "The charmed circle of lyric" is broken by the presence of "the kind of historical particularity that lyric genres exclude by design." Thus does the dramatic monologue "objectify" its subjective romantic inheritance; it "shows subjectivity up by betraying its situation in a history."[6] It does this—for example, in "My Last Duchess"—by laying out "the textual contradictions that constitute the Duke's character."[7]

This characteristic of Browning's dramatic monologues is what forces us to see them as models of the dialogical. A complex play of different voices arises in these texts because "one side of the verbal exchange has been silenced or suppressed" by the monological, not to say monomaniacal, speaker.[8] By imbedding that speaker and his text in a highly particularized historical context, the poem exposes "the conditional aspect of all utterances." Necessarily included in that exposure is the conditional aspect of those who produce readings of poems. The historicized particularity of the material "inside" the poem throws into relief the differential that appears through various particular readings. So the poem manages to "include [in itself] our own 'dramatic' situation as readers as well as the dramatic situation suggested by the text."[9]

AM.   But would you include Browning and Browning's own poems in that judgment of conditionality? Isn't it true that Browning and his poems "continue to posit an authority, albeit unknowable, behind the vagaries of the worldly frame of reference"?[10] That is to say, aren't poems like "Cleon" and "A Death in the Desert" and even *The Ring and the Book* "monological" and didactic?

GM.   Well, "Browning's earlier monologues (like "My Last Duchess") are more interesting than *The Ring and the Book* from the point of view of dialogism because they tend to make no explicit textual claims about their context or about a wider authorial context that might delimit their meanings." Of course, as readers "we are bound . . . by our own desire to contextualize authorial intentions as a part of history." But this only means that "we continue the process of dialogizing the text by adding our own perspectives."[11]

AM.   Don't be evasive. I was asking about *Browning's* ideological presence in his own work. You seem to acknowledge its presence, but then you remove it to the realm of the "unknowable" by saying that "author's intentions" are a construction of interpretive desire.

GM. Well, we can't really tell—in a poem like "My Last Duchess," for instance—what "Browning's" ideological intentions for the poem were.

AM. Because they "make no explicit textual claims about their context," etc.?

GM. Exactly. I wouldn't say the same of a poem like "Cleon" or *The Ring and the Book* even. But in "My Last Duchess" authorial intentions are invisible.

AM. Why not follow the logic of your own interpretive scheme—why not say that they enter the poem as one of its silenced voices? To me Browning's intentions seem the poem's strongest ideological presence exactly because they are the presence which the poem works hardest to silence and disguise.

JJR. As the Duke with the Duchess, as she with her lively feelings?

AM. Yes, but in each case the effort fails. The subtitle "Ferrara"[12] appears in the poem in the context of Browning's early-Victorian interest in the Italian Renaissance. As such, it carries very particular overtones of meaning. And in the first edition the work's bibliographical coding emphasized Browning's "intentions" toward his poem even more strongly. When "My Last Duchess" was paired with "Count Gismond," Browning's views about national psychological traits were explicitly being set forth, as well as his ideas about the proper relations of men and women. To me, both poems are nothing but little Victorian sermons.

GM. You can't be serious.

AM. I couldn't be *more* serious. "My Last Duchess," for instance, is largely constructed as a critique of aristocratic pride, which Browning associates with the desire to possess and control. The villainy is especially heinous, according to this poem, because of its object: an adorable woman. But note that the poem is completely uncritical in its association of the woman with beauty. Her value comes from her beauty—which is why the Duke has enshrined her in, and as, a work of art.

Implicit here is the notion—one finds it all over Browning's poetry—that life (as opposed to art) is a primary value, and that art's office is to celebrate and broadcast this primary value.

GM. Do you have any problem with that?

AM. I'm not devaluing the poem, I'm just reading it. But I *could* point out that some excellent readers—Baudelaire comes immediately to mind, and so does Lautréamont—would surely find Browning's sermon insufferable, and would just as surely choose to take the Duke's part.

But leaving that aside, I have to point out another implication of the poem. The Duke is judged harshly by the text because he wants to keep the Duchess to himself. This desire is seen as especially wicked because of the way the Duchess is presented: as a lovely and spontaneous creature who enjoys and is enjoyed by the company of all classes. Now this representation of the Duchess is not so different from the Duke's representation in one crucial respect: both take her as a thing of beauty that might be a joy forever, both take her—essentially—as an aesthetic image. The poem does not judge the Duke harshly for thinking her adorable—Browning's poetry never does that—but only for wishing to keep her for his private pleasure.

GM. In short, the poem seems to you sexist.

AM. No question about it. It's not a bad poem because of its sexism, of course. But it is *ideological* for that (and other) reasons—by which I simply mean it's a poem that makes moral representations which someone might reasonably acknowledge. . . .

JJR. And contest.

❧

JM. Sorry about that—the tape ran out. But I've put in a new one now, so let's go on.[d]

AM. Just as well too, that interruption. We started talking about dialogics and interpretation and then wandered off into Browning and the ideology of poetic form.

GM. But we also started with Bakhtin in our minds, and in his work dialogism is a function of the (primary) fictions, not of the (secondary) interpretations. Hermeneutics as dialogical is our appropriation of Bakhtin.

[d]This "event" in the dialogue is clearly of some importance, as Mack's discussion—now to come immediately—shows. All the interlocutors at this point turn reflexive.

AM.   Don't say "our," say "your." To me there is a sharp difference between the poetical and the interpretive field, though the two interact. But it is not a dialogical interaction because—as Socrates once pointed out to Protagoras—the texts of the poets don't talk to us.[13] We interrogate *them*. For their part—like Arnold's Shakespeare—they abide our question. Of course we can choose to imagine our primary texts as "intertexts" and thus treat them as if they were "dialogical." This is what Bakhtin does with novels, and he does it very well. But we should be clear about the metaphoric license he is taking when he treats fictional works as dialogical.

GM.   And so we find ourselves in a wonderfully Derridean situation. Interpretation—like this conversation of ours—is dialogical, and now reveals itself as the prior (substantive?) ground for the metaphoric extension of dialogics to fictional work and poetry.

JJR.   Composition as prior to inspiration?

GM.   Why not? It's simply another way of saying that scripture is philosophically prior to Logos.

JM.   May I ask a question? It may seem absurd, I realize, and somewhat beside the point of what you're talking about. But I don't see how we can *not* ask this question now that the conversation has completed a kind of Heideggerian circle.

    What *is* a dialogue? I have a tape in my hand with an electronic record of the first part of this conversation.[e] And as I listen to you talk, I watch the turning of the new spool, I watch a record being made of people talking. It makes me think a distinction has to be drawn somewhere that is not being drawn—perhaps a distinction between what we might call "conversation" on one hand and "dialogue" on the other.

    Maybe what we're doing now is not "dialogue." At any event, it seems very different from the following. Here, read this.

An ABC of Interdisciplinarity. A Dialogue
by Sheri Meghan

A.   As Moses Hadas always used to say: "The only interesting talk is shop talk."

[e] The text here is not based directly on the tape referred to by McGrem, but upon the printer's-copy typescript. The latter may or may not give an accurate and complete record of the original conversation. Our text appears to begin *in media res*, so it may not represent the whole of "the first part" of the conversation that was apparently on the tape McGrem mentions.

B. All shops are closed shops, more or less. Suffocating. If you're not a professor and you find yourself, by circumstance, dropped among a bunch of professors at lunch, how interesting do you imagine you'll find their conversation?

C. Well, suppose you came there as an ethnographer. Then the shoptalk might seem *very* interesting indeed.

A. But it wouldn't be shoptalk anymore, it would be ethnographic information. And if the professors were conscious of themselves as ethnographic subjects, even they would not be producing shoptalk any longer.

B. A blessed event, the coming of the ethnographer to the ingrown conversations of the closed shop. And more blessed still should she come to the smug halls of late twentieth-century academe. Enlightened halls, open—or so their citizens like to think—to every kind of talk.

A. And so they are.

B. Only if the talk is framed in a certain way. The academy is the scene where knowledge has been made an object of devotion. Its two gods, or two-personed god, are science (positive knowledge) and philology (the knowledge of what is known). It is a cognitive scene, a scene of calculations and reflections. It is the country for old men. Children, whether of woman or of Jesus born, do not come there—unless it be to leave behind their childlikeness.

C. They do not come because the knowledge of the childlike person is experiential rather than reflective.

B. Socrates in his trance, Alcibiades in his cups?

C. They will do nicely as signs of what both justifies and threatens every symposium, every state—the Outsiders that are within. Admired and hated, sought and feared; finally—because every state, every closed shop, is what it is—*expelled*.

B. And what then of your ethnographer, that darling of the modern academy? Is it not the ultimate dream of *Wissenschaft* that all things should submit to reflection, that experience itself should become—*fieldwork*? In the ancient world of Plato that sick dream appeared as the Socratic philosopher; more recently it came as the nightmare of the positive scientist, mystified forever in the figure of Wordsworth's Newton, "voyaging through strange seas of thought, alone." Mary Shelley lifted his mask and we glimpsed the haunted face as Victor Frankenstein, whose monstrous creature is the index of

Frankenstein's soul as it has been observed through the lens of an outsider's—in this case, a woman's—sense of the pitiful.

c.   So you don't care for ethnographers either.

b.   Well, they are our latest Faustian types. Benevolent colonialists. Today
their shoptalk—it is called Cultural Studies—has given the modern academy some of its most effective means of self-mystification. As if the academy could harbor within itself its own outsider, its own critical observer.

a.   That "critical observer" you are imagining is the real illusion. All observers
are inside the shop. If they weren't they wouldn't even know about the
shop, couldn't see it, and hence couldn't talk at all. Shoptalk is "interesting"
because people share their differences.

c.   So for you it's not merely that "the only interesting talk is shop talk"; more
than that, "Shop talk is all there is!"

a.   Exactly. But some shoptalk *is* more interesting than other shoptalk.

c.   And what makes it more interesting?

a.   Every shop has many conversations going on inside of it all the time. The
most interesting conversations are those that get everybody else talking—
talking about them, or talking in their terms.

b.   But where do those new and interesting conversations come from? Inside
the shop?

a.   Evidently.

c.   Why "evidently"? Is the rapt Socrates inside or outside? And what about
Alcibiades—drunk or sober? We all remember how, and where, he
died.

b.   Inside or outside, it doesn't matter. The point is that every shop must be
something *other* than what anyone, *inside or outside*, could think or imagine
it to be. The shop must be, in some sense, *beside itself.* Irrational. Other
than itsef. Otherwise it cannot accommodate—either conceptually *or* ex-
perientially—anything "new."

a.   Put it that way if you like. Shoptalk is often irrational. Just so you don't bore
us with ideas about absolute critical differentials.

b.   Have it so if *you* like. Just so you don't insult us with ideas about knowing
or accommodating otherness. No shop—no academy—can do so. Otherness comes like a wolf to a sheepfold. Later, when the damage is done,
the priests—let us say, the professors—will indulge their shoptalk of explanations.

JM. This dialogue was originally presented in the spring of 1990, at a conference on Herder that was held in Charlottesville, Virginia. Meghan presented it at a panel discussion that took up the (very Herderian) question of interdisciplinarity.

JJR. It seems to be a kind of position paper making an ironical critique of the form, or idea, of position papers as such. Perhaps in order to ask that critical reflection precede the taking of positions.

GM. Or perhaps to make a game of critical reflection as such. I was at the conference, Joanne, and I think you ought to tell everyone that the dialogue was *not* given by anyone named Sheri Meghan. It was written and delivered by Jerome McGann. Sheri Meghan is just a mask, like the dialogue's A, B, and C.

JM. I wasn't trying to conceal that fact. The masquerade is crucial.

GM. Maybe so, maybe not. But what about McGann? Was he just playing around, making a parade of cleverness.

AM. Right. If it's all just a masquerade, what's the point? The dialogue's ironies are pretty ingrown, after all. And look at the conclusion, where nothing is concluded: C stands altogether silent at that point, while A and B simply make a pair of smart, dismissive remarks.

JM. You're all missing my point. I ask again: What is a dialogue; what is *this* dialogue? Or suppose I ask: *where* is it? Right now we're been reading it as a printed text. In 1990 it was delivered orally by McGann (in his Meghan masquerade) at the Herder conference. It seems the dialogue is not at all the same thing under those two different conditions. When it was orally presented, it was—surely— part of McGann's way of taking a position—whatever that position was, however we define it.

GM. The position of not taking a position?

JM. If that's what he was doing, it's a position. But let me set your question aside for a moment—only for a moment, I promise. Whatever McGann was doing at the Herder conference, here the dialogue has become part of *my* taking a position. Those two positions—whatever they are—may be symmetrical, but they probably aren't. At least they don't seem so to me. I introduced McGann's text here because

I wanted to interrogate the idea of dialogue—or get all of us to investigate it—in a different perspective.

It's the tape machine that set me thinking this way. Here we're talking and there our words are being gathered and edited—and turned into something entirely new. I want to say this: they are being translated from conversation into dialogue.

GM. Of course—because they're being given a secondary—as it were a *literary*—form.

JM. But that simple change appears to make a world of difference.

JJR. How much of a difference depends upon how much "editing" is done. Joanne's tape machine is making a sound record of our conversation. But that record leaves out the whole visual element. Besides, the machine is such a primitive mechanism that even the oral record it might deliver will be deficient. If you've ever tried to translate an audiotape into a typescript, you'll know what I mean. Without the visual element, the raw phonic record often seems clumsy and difficult to understand. Besides, unless you have multiple sound devices—at least one focused on each speaker individually, and perhaps others as well—you'll find it difficult to recover exactly what was said.

Or suppose we had set up a fixed video camera that made an audiovisual record of these conversations. The output of that camera would not display much "literary form." But if we used, say, four cameras, and had them manually operated, the situation changes drastically. Under those conditions you would need various mechanisms of coordination, and ultimately both a director and an editor. The output would not be a "record of our conversations," it would be a work of artistic and editorial translation.

It takes little effort to see that a similar set of differentials applies if the translation carries the original conversation into a traditional literary form. The dialogues of Plato, Diderot, and Wilde are artistic and editorial constructions. Indeed, in those cases the distance between "original conversations" and literary output seems so great—so absolute even—that we regard their texts as dialogical inventions.

AM. Once again those necessary fictions, apparently.

JJR. Not at all. I should rather call them *un*necessary fictions. No necessity called them into being. They had to be arbitrarily, deliberately *made.* In a sense, they have no "origin" at all; if any "conversational moment" once lay behind them, the translation process is so complete as to have (as it were) erased it forever from the record. (By the way, Anne, that's another metaphor!)

AM. Yes, and one that wouldn't apply to what's going on here—should Joanne's taped record ever find its way into editorial hands.

JJR. Of course.

JM. But why not?

AM. Well obviously because the ultimate "dialogue"—I use your term for such a work—has become the entire focus of attention. Dialogue exists in and as a "secondary world." To the degree that it has been successfully executed—say in Plato, Diderot, or Wilde—to that extent the work has changed, changed utterly. The record has been lost in the birth of beauty.

GM. Which is not such a terrible thing.

JM. Ever so clever, Georg—but what's the point? That "conversation" is "real," whereas "dialogue" is "imaginary"? What kind of trivial distinction is that?

Suppose we think about it this way: that every secondary world, every mimetic construction, comes to us under the watchful eyes of its recording angel. Isn't this what the ancients meant when they said that memory is the mother of the muses?

Let us assume that the splendid dialogues of Oscar Wilde have no originary "conversational moment." Let us assume, in other words, that they neither carry nor erase the memory of such a moment. Let us assume they are pure inventions. Even so, they cannot escape their recording angel. For they will always be a record of themselves. Even as pure invention they set down a documentary record of what went into the construction of their fictionality.[f]

Nor must we imagine that this documentary moment must be separated from the fictional moment. Such an abstract separation can be made for special analytic purposes. Whatever the usefulness of the abstraction, it will obscure and confuse the record that the fiction is making of itself—and hence will obscure and confuse the fiction.

[f] None of Joanne McGrem's interlocutors queried her on this point. But one would like to know if she meant that the documentary record is complete. To us, such completion seems hardly possible.

GM.   I don't understand exactly what you're talking about, Joanne. What is this idea about fiction making a record of itself?

JM.   Simply that all imaginative work appears to us in specific material forms. Many people—even many textual scholars—don't realize the *imaginative* importance of those material forms. Blake's work forcibly reminds us that the way poems are printed and distributed is part of their meaning. That process of printing and distribution is essential to "the record that fiction makes of itself." It locates the imagination socially and historically. When Emily Dickinson decided not to publish her poems, when she decided to gather her handwritten texts into a series of "little books" which she kept to herself, those acts and their material forms comprise part of the record her work makes of itself. They are a crucial framework which Dickinson constructed for making her meanings, and which we need if we are to understand and respond.

I could give you similar examples from all the writers I know well. Which is why I say that a recording angel presides over the transcendental imagination—whether it be a poetical or a critical imagination. Her descent to earth in the twentieth century came, as usual, in masquerade. She once appeared, for example, as Bertolt Brecht, whose great project was to reestablish the theatrical unity of knowledge and pleasure, truth and beauty, instruction and entertainment. His guiding principle—it took many practical material forms—was what he called "the alienation effect." In Brecht's "epic theatre"

> the spectator was no longer in any way allowed to submit to an experience uncritically (and without practical consequences) by means of simple empathy with the characters in the play. The production took the subject matter and incidents shown and put them through a process of alienation: the alienation necessary to all understanding.[14]

Brecht wanted to encourage the audience's critical awareness of the entire fictional presentation. To do this required that the theatrical event be, as it were, documented at the very moment of its dramatization. "Footnotes, and the habit of turning back to check a point, need to be introduced into playwriting" in order to break the hypnotizing spell of aesthetic space, where spectators (or readers) are not encouraged "to think *about* a subject, but within the confines of the subject."[15]

Brecht called his project "epic theatre" because it introduced what he called a "narrative" element into the dramatic space. This narrative documents what is happening on the stage, adds footnotes to the action, supplies references.

> The stage began to tell a story. The narrator was no longer missing, along with the fourth wall. Not only did the background adopt an attitude to the events on the stage—by big screens recalling other simultaneous events elsewhere, by projecting documents which confirmed or contradicted what the characters said, by concrete and intelligible figures to accompany abstract conversations, by figures and sentences to support mimed transactions whose sense was unclear—but the actors too refrained from going over wholly into their role, remaining detached from the character they were playing and clearly inviting criticism of him.[16]

Now it seems to me that dialogue might be distinguished from conversation along similar lines. Dialogue puts conversation in a literary frame, and by doing this it documents its own activities: literally, gives them a local habitation and a set of names.[g]

GM.   There's nothing especially novel about all this. What you are describing is just the "moment of reflection" which hermeneutics has always recognized in literary work. It is the moment which interpretation seeks to extend and develop through the (re)generation of meanings.

JJR.   No, it is much more than that. Brecht's (or is it Joanne's?) recording angel operates according to Feuerbach's eleventh thesis, where the point is not simply to "interpret the world" but to "change it." Brechtian theatrics are socialist and polemical throughout—as we see in the following passage, which Joanne did *not* choose to quote, even though it is the continuation of one of the texts she was reading to us. Brecht distinguishes between the (old, passive) "dramatic" theatre and the (new, engaged) "epic" theater:

> The dramatic theatre's spectator says: Yes, I have felt like that too— Just like me—Only natural—It'll never change—The sufferings of this man appal me, because they are inescapable—That's great art . . . —I weep when they weep, I laugh when they laugh.

[g] At this point one might hazard the following descriptions of the different positions being taken in the dialogue. Mannejc sees interpretation as dialogue; Rome sees criticism (critique) as dialogic; Mack seems to regard poetry, or imaginative writing generally, as dialogical; and finally McGrem turns the distinction completely around and argues that dialogue is poetry, or at any rate that it is a noninformational form of discourse.

The epic theatre's spectator says: I'd never have thought it—
That's not the way . . . —It's got to stop—The sufferings of this
man appal me, because they are unnecessary—That's great art . . .
—I laugh when they weep, I weep when they laugh.[17]

Brecht's documentation is not positivist—a matter of keeping good
records; it is interventionist. The recording angel is a figure of judgment and even apocalypse, a figure come to reveal secrets of good
and evil that have been hidden, if not from the beginning of time, at
least throughout human history. The angel opens up the book of a
new life, turns the world upside down. The outcome is anything but
the pluralist heaven of hermeneutics.

GM.   Well, you could have fooled me. Here I am talking in a dialogue that
labels itself as such, in the best Brechtian fashion. Joanne makes a
parade of her self-consciousness about dialogues and conversations;
she wonders "what" a dialogue is, "where" it is? But what and where
am I? Surely I am plunged in the very "heaven (or hell) of hermeneutics" itself—a paradise of pluralism and shoptalk.

I mean, whose play are we acting in here? Joanne tells us in a
charming metaphor that "a recording angel" made "her descent to
earth . . . in masquerade." But all this is no metaphor, my friends. All
this *is* a masquerade! Let's set the record straight about that at any
rate. Let's add another Brechtian label and get everything out front.
We'll call this "The Puppet Theater of Jerome McGann."

JEROME MCGANN.   Did you think I was trying to conceal myself? Surely
it's been evident right along that all of this—you four in particular—
are what Blake used to call the vehicular forms of (my) imagination.
Masquerade allows us to turn concealment into purest apparition. It
is manifest deception.

GM.   Fair enough, but then what is this masquerade all about, what are
you trying to get across? You may *say* you're not trying to conceal
yourself, but you let us go on arguing and discussing different ideas
and we begin to forget all about you. We even begin to think that we
are different—different from each other, different from you. But
we're not, we all come out of the same rag and bone shop.

JEROME MCGANN.   Well, just knowing that is pretty interesting. Especially
today when "the star of Bakhtin has risen in the West." People and
texts are supposed to be the repositories of conflicting voices—or at

any rate different voices. Rainbow coalitions and so forth. Richness in diversity. But there is always (what did Ashbery call it?) a "Plainness in Diversity" and it's just as well to be aware of it, don't you think?

GM. Who cares what *I* think—"I" don't think at all! The question is, what do *you* think?

JEROME MCGANN. I think you're more involved in thinking than you realize.

GM. I'm just a textual construct.

JEROME MCGANN. So you say—a puppet in a puppet theater. Whereas I'm flesh and blood, of course.

AM. Sometimes I think we have more life than we realize—or at least that we might have more.

> Thou wert not born for death, immortal bird,
> No hungry generations tread thee down.

I'm that bird, I think. What did Shakespeare write?

> Not marble nor the gilded monuments
> Of princes shall outlive this pow'rful rhyme.

Flesh and blood is all very well, but texts have their own advantages.

GM. We don't think, we have no identities. *He* does. Whatever we do is done for us. Someone will read me and tell me what I mean. It's true that different people might make me mean different things. We've all been told about the openness of the text and the freedom of the reader. But what do *I* care about reader responses? They make us seem little more than empty tablets, waiting to be written on.

JEROME MCGANN. As I said, I think you're more involved in thinking than you realize.

GM. What are you getting at?

JEROME MCGANN. Thinking only gets carried out in language, in texts. We sometimes imagine that we can think outside of language—for instance, in our heads, where we don't exteriorize the language we're using in language's customary (oral or scripted) forms. But the truth is that all thought is linguistically formed. Even mathematicians think about their abstract worlds in material languages.

You whine about being a textual construct. But you're able to think for precisely that reason. And so am I, and so are we all. We're all textual constructs.

GM. What sophistry.

JM. On the contrary, what truth! We really do think because we are textual constructs, and we do so because thinking is the play of different ideas, the testing of the limits and the possibilities of ideas. Why complain that this masquerade seems, in one perspective, a professor's monologue? It's not the only way to see it. In *any* case we're testing limits and possibilities.

GM. No *we're* not. *He* is—if anyone is.

JM. What about someone listening to all this, or reading it?

GM. Sure, but they're flesh and blood too. It's people who think, not texts, not the masks that people fashion and put on.

JEROME MCGANN. But my idea is that texts are the flesh and blood of thought—that in language we are all masked creatures who act in masquerades. I've written this dialogue—constructed even an ingrate like yourself—to pursue that thought, or perhaps I should say to have it pursued—finally to be pursued by it.

Take yourself, for instance. You're always surprising me. You think you're just a puppet, but the truth is that I often don't know what you or I or anybody else here might do or say next. This whole last five minutes of conversation we're having. I never planned it, never even thought about it until a friend of mine read what you called my puppet theater and queried its masquerade in ways I hadn't thought about. And then she challenged me about it, and we talked back and forth, and I came back at last to you. And so I started writing some more—writing what we're arguing about now.

How did those changes happen? There's a writer—let's call him me; and there's a reader—my friend; and then there's all of us, we textual constructs. Don't we have any responsibility in this masquerade?

AM. But you're not one of us! And the answer is no, *we* don't. The responsibility is all yours, yours and your friend's, and all the other (re)writers and (re)readers of texts.

But I agree with you in this much anyhow: we aren't blank tablets or empty signs. We're characters, we have histories. If masks are disguises, they take particular forms. It makes a big difference what face you put on when you engage in masquerade.

JEROME MCGANN. So, Georg, don't ask *me* what I think about all this. Interrogate the masks if you want to know that. The question is not: "Why do you move in masquerade?" We all do. The question is: "Why does your masquerade take the form that it does? Why these characters and not others?"

AM. But there are other questions as well. Odd as it might seem, Jerome, one might not be especially interested in what you thought about this dialogue, or what you had in mind for it. The dialogue isn't yours, isn't even your friend's. This place lies east of Eden where we—what did you call us?—"textual constructs" seek a life of our own—in fact, seek many lives of our own. All texts do.

Bakhtin used to say that novels were dialogical but poems were monological. But he was wrong in this. In a sense, poetry is far more "dialogical" (in Bakhtin's sense) than fiction just because poetry asks us to pay attention to the word-as-such, to focus on the text *as it is a textual construct.* Poetry thus makes us aware of the masquerade that is being executed by even the most apparently transparent and authoritative texts. By this text, for instance—Robert Frost's well-known jingoist lyric "The Gift Outright."

> The land was ours before we were the land's.
> She was our land more than a hundred years
> Before we were her people. She was ours,
> In Massachusetts, in Virginia,
> But we were England's, still colonials,
> Possessing what we still were unpossessed by,
> Possessed by what we now no more possessed.
> Something we were withholding made us weak
> Until we found out that it was ourselves
> We were withholding from our land of living.
> Such as we were we gave ourselves outright
> (The deed of gift was many deeds of war)
> To the land vaguely realizing westward,
> But still unstoried, artless, unenhanced,
> Such as she was, such as she would become.

That was written during the height of the Second World War—a pretty piece of patriotism. But the text says much more than it realizes because language always stands in a superior truth to those who use the language. Blood spilled in this poem's land becomes the sign of the right of possession. But who is the "we" of this poem; what are those "many deeds of war"?

One word in this text—"Massachusetts"—reminds us that this supremely Anglo-American poem cannot escape or erase a history that stands beyond its white myth of Manifest Destiny. That central New England place, Massachusetts, is rooted in Native American soil and language, where the very idea of being possessed by land—rather than possessing it or conquering it in martial struggles—finds its deepest truth and expression. Unlike "Virginia," "Massachusetts" is Native American, red-skinned. Colonized by another culture and language, that word (which is also a place and a people, red before it could ever be white) preserves its original testimony and truth;[h] and when it enters this poem, it tilts every white word and idea into another set of possible meanings and relations. "Virginia," for example, which is a lying, European word[i]—a word whose concealments are suddenly exposed when it finds itself in a united (poetical) state with "Massachusetts." When *I* read this poem, those "many deeds of war" include the Indian Wars that moved inexorably "westward." In this poem, I think, all blood is originally red. "Virginia"? Not at all. She was already married, and then she was raped. That is what this text tells us, unbeknownst to Robert Frost, yet redeeming, to a degree, his blindness.

Where do such different voices come from? Language speaks through us, and language, like Tennyson's sea, moans round with many voices. In "The Gift Outright" we see how some voices come unbidden—come, indeed, as outright gifts so far as the intentionality of the authored work is concerned. Because the poem's rhetoric is preponderantly and unmistakably Euro-American, "Massachusetts" sends out only a faint signal of the (otherwise great) hidden history the word involves. And it is important that we see the signal come so faintly and obliquely—so undeliberately, as it were—when we read the poem. The faintness is the sign of

[h] The word names the tribe which ranged the Boston area, and it means something like "near the great hill." The reference is, apparently, to the Great Blue Hill south of the city.

[i] I believe the phrase "a lying, European word" must be an allusion to Laura Riding's great poem "Poet: A Lying Word" (the title piece in the volume *Poet: A Lying Word* [London: Arthur Barker Ltd., 1933] 129–34). In the context of Frost's poem, the word "Virginia" is radically deceitful (or perhaps "self-deceived") precisely because of what the word's root meaning intends to suggest about "the land" that would be taken over from others in order to be translated into the Commonwealth of Virginia

important historical relations of cultural dominance and cultural marginality. The whole truth of those relations, imbedded in this text, would not be able to appear if Frost had not given his white, European mythology over to his poem's language, where it finds a measure of release from its own bondage. A measure of release.

This is why I care about what you think, Jerome—and also about what you *don't think* to think. Because you're one among many—in the end, one of us. As you say, a textual construct.

JEROME MCGANN.   "Zooks, Sir! Flesh and blood, that's all I'm made of."

Afterword

Ceci n'est pas une pipe.

—René Magritte

I CLOSE THIS BOOK with some brief comments on literalness as a feature of the language of modernism. While these remarks may seem (perhaps even contemptuously) familiar to linguists, they may be useful for students of literature and culture, who often continue to think about modernism in conceptual terms drawn from romanticism. The language of modernism, however—which we still use today, though the dialect is dominantly *post*modern—is drastically modified, and often turned away altogether, from romantic paradigms of language. This shift can be marked even in the most "romantic" of the modernists—even, that is to say, in writers like Yeats, as we have seen.

In a recent paper Gabor Bezeczky spins out an elegant deconstruction of the idea of a "literal language."[1] Making a logical march through "all the forces and factors" that would render a language unstable, Bezeczky shows that to remove them—an operation necessary for the establishment of perfect literalness as Bezeczky conceives it—would entail "the destruction of words" as such (610). His witty conclusion is not merely that "literal language in its ideal form seems to be nonexistent"; he adds—correctly, given his premises—that "a similar reductive argument could also be applied to 'metaphorical language'" (610).

Bezeczky's demonstration is designed as an indirect argument in favor of Paul Ricoeur's "venturesome hypothesis" about the relation of literalness to metaphor. Regarding metaphor as "an heuristic of thought,"[2] Ricoeur leads Bezeczky to the conclusion that literalness is a function of metaphoricity: "Words in their normal, literal use may not exist without similarity but the perception of similarity cannot be stopped from being creative" (610). A kind of symbiosis (not really a dialectic) operates between the literal and the metaphorical. Metaphor is the driving energy (or motor) of language, and literalness is one phase or moment in metaphor's generative operations.

But of course this conclusion could itself be deconstructed along Bezeczky's lines since it assumes the literal existence of metaphor as "an heuristic of thought." A mere slight of mind partly obscures the continuity of Bezeczky's logical paradoxes (as we see by asking simply: What is the linguistic status of a phrase like "an heuristic of thought"?). The problem with (as well as the power and usefulness of) this whole approach to the study of language is a function of its synchronic and formal horizon. Bezeczky's "reductive argument" (610), for example, assumes that words are the basic units of language, and that an "ideally literal language" is necessarily—by definition, really—one that is "standard and self-contained" (609). For Bezeczky, there are on one hand "literal languages" (or the conceptual possibilities of such) and on the other "natural languages," and the two "cannot resemble" each other (609). (This position entails as well that there are "metaphorical languages" and "natural languages" which must be equally incommensurable.) But the whole structure is a kind of hall of mirrors. If metaphor is "an heuristic of thought," then literalness must also be conceived as such. Furthermore, we have no way of distinguishing (logically) the status of the terms "metaphor" and "literalness": are they "literal" or are they "metaphoric"?

The picture changes when we approach language along rhetorical and constructivist lines. When the horizon of our thinking is "the meaning is the use," new possibilities of "literalness" appear. Within this alternative horizon, the following (paradoxical) sentence might be regarded as an exemplary form:

This is not a sentence.

The important feature of this sentence is its self-citation. It deploys a (conceptual) paradox that is commensurate with its linguistic form. The paradox is important because it highlights the constructedness of the "sentence." Here we see how a "sentence" may be far more than a "sentence" and yet remain, linguistically, a "sentence"—however we define that (multiply definable) term. In addition—given the "context" in which the sentence has been placed—the words (implicitly) construct an argument about the nature of language where the form of the argument—the environment which is this book—serves as example, or demonstration, of the idea.

In this perspective, the "literalness" of language is not only *not* "nonexistent," it is one of language's permanent features. The formal and semantic elements of language can only appear in a rhetorical or performative condition.

Here is another exemplary instance of (really, index to) the literalness of language:

> I give you my word.

In contrast to "this is not a sentence," paradox here does not function as the performative locus of literalness. The sentence illustrates one of the most traditional rhetorics (the promise) where self-identity makes its linguistic appearance. In the present context, of course, the words do not function as a promise but as an example of linguistic literalness. So the words here "mean" something other than what they might (and do) otherwise and traditionally "mean."

Despite this difference in "meaning"—and the differential is *part of the meaning of the words as they are being used here*—these words retain their literalness. They function not as promise but as example. And they are a *particular* example. In their immediate context, they argue (demonstrate?) that a "promise" can and must be (latently) more than a promise even as it remains literally a "promise." It is as well, literally, something else again.

Promises are more than promises, examples more than examples, and the same can be said of statements, propositions, metaphors, what have you. Indeed, it is the *literalness* of these things (not at all their metaphoricity) which opens them to their many transformational possibilities. The phrase "I give you my word," whether as promise or as example, clearly involves a metaphor; but it is the (given, literal) deployment of the metaphor, the way it is used (and taken to be used), that structures the action of the language.

> I said, "I give you my word."
> He gave you his word.
> He gave her his word.

The last example illustrates words being employed (literally) in a report or narrative form. In all these instances, the stable element (as it were) is the metaphor, whereas the literal element undergoes constant transformation. What does not change, however, as the poet said, is the will to change.

In modernist writing, aesthetic space begins to turn into writing space. The "novel" as a self-contained narrative continuum gets framed in a writing structure that calls attention to the writing's "novelism" or "narrativity." We move not so much in a symbolic medium as a rhetorical medium that has as one of its resources "symbolic form." Practically any work of modernism could be used to illustrate this feature of modernist textuality.

This characteristic of modernism signals its will to change from certain of its inherited (romantic) traditions. The present book has been exploring one special set of resources that modernist cultural change exploited and pursued. Beginning with Morris, writers were "going crazy about typographical form," as Williams put it, because they were exploring the transformational resources of language as a literal event (an event of letters). The psychological and symbolic explorations of language carried out in the romantic tradition had left the acoustic and visual aspects of language—the physique of its meanings—badly neglected. Pursuing the rhetoric of "sincerity" as if it were an escape from rhetoric, nineteenth-century writers had also neglected the rhetorical resources of language. An aggressive turn to the literal began with the Pre-Raphaelites and was continued by the so-called aesthetes of the 1890s.

I have spent most of this book focusing on these revolutions of the word as they appeared in their most visible forms. Were we to trace out a similar history in the development of modern rhetoric away from the (expended) conventions of sincerity, Oscar Wilde would come center stage, as would that other forgotten cultural resource, the writing of the immediate romantic aftermath, the writing of (approximately) 1820–1832. These interesting topics fall outside the perspective of the present work. Indeed, the study of Wilde and the 1820s relates to modernism more through postmodern analogues and avenues than through modernist ones.

We shall not be able to redraw the map of modernism—so badly in need of doing—without a great reconstruction of "modern memory."[3] This book tells only one small part of a much larger story.

Notes

PREFACE

1. *The Levinas Reader*, ed. Sean Hand (Oxford: Basil Blackwood, 1989), 134.

2. An indispensable point of departure for investigating the future of the book in the age of media and electronics is the Collected Research Reports of the Toronto Research Group, just reprinted as *Rational Geomancy*, by Steve McCaffery and bpNichol, ed. Steve McCaffery (Vancouver: Talonbooks, 1992).

INTRODUCTION

1. My text is from *W. B. Yeats. The Poems* (revised), ed. Richard J. Finneran (New York: Macmillan, 1989), 346–48.

2. See W. H. Auden, *Secondary Worlds. Essays by W. H. Auden* (New York: Random House, 1968), 135.

3. *W. B. Yeats. The Poems*, ed. Daniel Albright (London: J. M. Dent and Sons, 1990), 844.

4. The standard discussion of the process of composition is in Curtis B. Bradford's *Yeats at Work* (Carbondale and Edwardsville, Ill.: Southern Illinois University Press, 1965), 157–67.

5. I here use the reprint with a new introduction by John D. Rosenberg (New York: Dover Publications, 1968), 2:104–42.

6. The best rag paper was made from white linen rags, "while coloured linens, canvas, old rope, and even a proportion of woolens went into the poorer qualities" (Philip Gaskell, *A New Introduction to Bibliography* [Oxford: Oxford University Press, 1972], 66). Before the use of wood pulp became possible (late in the nineteenth century), various other materials were tried, including cotton rags.

7. See Gaskell, *A New Introduction*, 223–24.

8. See Will Ransom, *Private Presses and their Books* (New York: R. R. Bowker and Co., 1929), who points out that "an Albion press, Caslon type, and all-rag paper made in Ireland (though not hand made) is all the equipment" at the Cuala Press (p. 92). See also Robin Skelton, "Twentieth-Century Irish Literature and the Private Press Tradition: *Dun Emer, Cuala, & Dolmen Presses* 1902 1963," *The Massachusetts Review* 5 (Winter 1964): especially 370–71. In fact the paper was manufactured at Saggart Mills, County Dublin.

9. See Liam Miller, *The Dun Emer Press, later the Cuala Press . . .* , Preface by Michael B. Yeats (New York: The Typophiles, 1974); and Ransom, *Private Presses*, and Skelton, "Twentieth-Century Irish Literature."

10. Cuala Press came into being in 1908, when the Yeats sisters separated from Dun Emer Industries, which had been founded by Evelyn Gleeson. For details see Liam Miller, "The Dun Emer and the Cuala Press," in *The World of W. B. Yeats*, ed. Robin Skelton and Ann Saddlemyer, rev. ed. (New York: University of Washington Press, 1967), 111–133, especially 112–14; and Lisa Unger Baskin, "A Gathering from the Dun Emer Press and the Cuala Press," *Massachusetts Review* 28 (Autumn 1987): 525–49.

11. See Skelton, "Twentieth-Century Irish Literature," 369, and 370–71.

12. See Gaskell, *A New Introduction*; and for more comprehensive treatments of these matters see Sir Albert Dykes Spicer, *The Paper Trade* (London: Methuen Inc., 1907); Richard Leslie Hills, *Papermaking in Britain, 1488–1988* (London: Athlone, 1988).

13. See Curtis Bradford, *Yeats at Work* (Carbondale and Edwardsville, Ill.: Southern Illinois University Press, 1965), 164.

14. Finneran gives the history of publication in *Editing Yeats's Poems. A Reconsideration* (London: Macmillan, 1990), 78–87; see also 122–23 for particular discussion of "The Circus Animals' Desertion."

15. See *The Letters of W. B. Yeats*, ed. Allan Wade (reprinted by Octagon Books: New York, 1980), 397–98; see also 381, 404–5.

16. See *The Collected Letters of W. B. Yeats, 1865–1895*, ed. John Kelly and Eric Domville, Vol. 1 (Oxford: Clarendon Press, 1986), 403, 407, 434.

17. For a good discussion of this subject see Edward O'Shea, *Yeats as Editor* (Dublin: Dolmen Press, 1975), 36–56, especially 36–41. Typically Dun Emer/Cuala Press books were slim volumes issued in runs of 200 to 400 copies; they sold for around 10s.

18. For good treatments of these and related matters see R. D. Brown, "The Bodley Head Press: Some Bibliographical Extrapolations," *Papers of the Bibliographical Society of America* 61 (1967): 39–50; and James G. Nelson, *The Early Nineties. A View from the Bodley Head* (Cambridge, Mass.: Harvard University Press, 1970). See also the recent essay by Margaret Diane Stetz, "Sex, Lies, and Printed Cloth: Bookselling at the Bodley Head in the Eighteen-Nineties," *Victorian Studies* 35 (Autumn 1991): 71–86, especially 73–74.

19. See E. P. Thompson, "The Communism of William Morris: A Lecture" (London: William Morris Society, 1965), 9.

20. The phrase sounds like a rubric for modernism. In fact it is John M. Munro's description of what held together the wildly diverse cultural aspects of the 1890s scene (in *English Poetry in Transition, 1880–1920* (New York: Pegasus, 1968), 26.

21. My discussion of Stein's publication history owes a deep debt to the work of El Warner. See her Ph.D. thesis *"Officer, She's Writing Again!" Gertrude Stein and her Reception* (Charlottesville: University of Virginia, 1992).

22. For an interesting early critical estimate of Evans see Cornwall Hollis's pamphlet *The Art of Donald Evans* (Philadelphia: Nicholas L. Brown, n.d.).

23. See Eliot's review "Charleston, Hey! Hey!" *The Nation & Athenaeum* (29 January 1927), 595. Eliot published one piece by Stein in his *Criterion*. It was not a work to his liking, however.

24. It was first published in 1956 as the sixth volume of The Yale Edition of the

Unpublished Writings of Gertrude Stein: *Stanzas in Meditation and Other Poems (1929–1933)*, with a preface by Donald Sutherland (New Haven: Yale University Press, 1956).

25. See Spicer's brilliant review-essay "The Poems of Emily Dickinson," *The Boston Public Library Quarterly* 8 (July 1956): 135–43.

26. (Cambridge, Mass.: Belknap Press, 1981) 2 vols.

27. (Cambridge, Mass.: Belknap Press, 1955) 3 vols.

28. Millicent Todd Bingham, *Ancestors' Brocades* (New York: Harper, 1945), 17.

29. Franklin is now editing a new typographical edition of the poems.

30. In my commentaries here I follow the lead of Susan Howe, who has done more to advance our understanding of Dickinson's texts than anyone else. See her essay "These Flames and Generosities of the Heart: Emily Dickinson and the Illogic of Sumptuary Values," *Sulfur* 28 (Spring 1991): 134–55. Two of Howe's students (both from SUNY, Buffalo) are continuing and extending her work in the most significant ways: Marta Werner, who is completing her thesis on Dickinson's late fragments; and Jeanne Holland (now at University of Wyoming), whose recent paper given at a textual conference at Texas A & M, "Scraps, Stamps, and Cut-Outs: Emily Dickinson's Domestic Technologies of Publication," will be published soon in a collection of papers given at the conference.

31. There are also cases (very few) where one discerns numbers used to signal variants.

CHAPTER I

1. The fuller form of the imprint, naming Chiswick Press, also appears in the magazine, in the equivalent position at the end of each issue. Also noteworthy is the fact that Morris's next publication, *The Life and Death of Jason* (1867), was issued by Bell and Daldy and printed at Chiswick Press. At that point Morris switched publishers, turning to F. S. Ellis (whose printers were the unremarkable Strangeways and Walden).

2. For a good presentation of the operations of Chiswick Press see Janet Ing, "A London Shop of the 1850s: The Chiswick Press," *The Papers of the Bibliographical Society of America* 80 (1986): 153–78. See also below, nn. 4 and 10.

3. The magazine was the joint project of Morris and several of his Oxford friends, including Edward Burne-Jones, William Fulford, Wilfred Heeley, and Cormell Price. Many others contributed to the magazine, including D. G. Rossetti, but its conception, management, and editing came from the initial group of five young men. See Philip Henderson, *William Morris. His Life, Work, and Friends* (London: Thames and Hudson, 1967), especially 32–34.

4. For a good discussion of the type fonts of Chiswick Press see Janet Ing Freeman, "Founders' Type and Private Founts at the Chiswick Press in the 1850s," *Journal of the Printing Historical Society* nos. 19/20 for 1984/86, pp. 63–102. See also below, n. 10.

5. *The Oxford and Cambridge Magazine* (January 1856), 29.

6. Ibid., 31.

7. In Morris's work, the "right time" is love time, whatever the natural season. We see this clearly in the poems that deal with seasonal materials in *A Book of Verse*. So far as love is concerned, there is a time for every purpose under heaven—at least this is the law governing Morris's imagination. Of course love time is often a time of sorrow and unhappiness, loss and despair; but for Morris, love is not devalued because it brings suffering. On the contrary, in fact. See, for example, in *A Book of Verse*, the poems "Hope Dieth Love Liveth" and "Praise of Venus."

8. By the ballad conventions invoked in the poem, "*you*" is structurally male, just as "there" is structurally female. Needless to say, these are textual and not sexual categories.

9. This is the name now often given to the massive project for an illustrated edition of *The Earthly Paradise* which Morris planned in the late 1860s with his friend Burne-Jones. See Joseph R. Dunlap, *The Book that Never Was* (New York: Oriole Editions, 1971).

10. The old-face Caslon font was cut in 1844 for the Chiswick Press at the special request of Charles Whittingham. Its most distinctive feature is an elongated "s." (See *Chiswick Press. Interesting Information for those who Appreciate the Importance of this Famous Press in the History of Printing* (London: Chiswick Press, 1932). For an excellent general introduction to the bibliographical aspects of Morris's work see *William Morris and the Art of the Book* (New York: Pierpont Morgan Library and Oxford University Press, 1976), especially the essay by John Dreyfus "William Morris: Typographer," 71–96.

11. *The Ideal Book. Essays and Lectures on the Arts of the Book by William Morris*, ed. William S. Peterson (Berkeley and Los Angeles: University of California Press, 1982), 67.

12. Henderson, *William Morris*, 115.

13. The quotations here are all taken from Joyce Irene Whalley's introduction to the Scolar Press facsimile edition of *A Book of Verse* (London, 1981), p. [xi].

14. It is important to realize that the long lines of texts like these are not always allowed to break the frame. In "Love Alone," for example, some words break out while others are folded back in.

15. See his *The Kelmscott Press and William Morris Master-Craftsman* (London: Macmillan and Co., 1924), 53.

16. See *The Books of William Morris* (London: Frank Hollings, 1897), 140.

17. See William S. Peterson, "The Type-designs of William Morris," *Journal of the Printing Historical Society* nos. 19/20 for 1984/86, pp. 5–62; see especially p. 5.

CHAPTER 2

1. The essay was first printed in *The Contemporary Review* (October 1906); I quote here from the reprinted text in *Plays and Controversies* (London: Macmillan, 1923), 164–88; the quoted passage is at 170.

2. See Basil Bunting, *Collected Poems*, 2d ed. (Oxford: Oxford University Press, 1978), 110.

3. See Humphrey Carpenter, *A Serious Character. The Life of Ezra Pound* (London: Faber & Faber, 1988), 52.

4. See H. D.'s *End to Torment*, Norman Holmes Pearson and Michael King, eds. (New York: New Directions, 1979), where the text of the book is reprinted. It is interesting to note in passing that Yeats too was led by his Pre-Raphaelite inheritance to the production of a similar handmade book early in his career—one he made for Maude Gonne.

5. For further details on these early installments on the *Cantos*, and on other related bibliographical features of Pound's work, see my *The Textual Condition* (Princeton: Princeton University Press, 1991), chaps. 6–8 *passim*, especially 122–24, 130–38.

6. For an excellent discussion of Morris and his projects in decorative printing see Norman Kelvin, "Patterns in Time: The Decorative and the Narrative in the Work of William Morris," in *Nineteenth-Century Lives. Essays Presented to Jerome Hamilton Buckley*, ed. Lockridge, Maynard, and Stone (Cambridge: Cambridge University Press, 1989), 140–68. See also Henry Halliday Sparling's classic *The Kelmscott Press and William Morris Master-Craftsman* (London: Macmillan, 1924). Pound's initial serious involvement with Morris and his ideas continued during the time he worked with A. R. Orage and *The New Age*, for whom Morris was a central intellectual resource. See Tim Redman, *Ezra Pound and Fascism* (Cambridge and New York: Cambridge University Press, 1990), chap. 1, especially pp. 21–22.

7. Zukofsky elaborated the distinction in an essay he wrote for the 1932 anthology's precursor text, the special February 1931 issue of *Poetry*, which he guest edited as another objectivist collection.

8. In this connection, Dickinson's connection to emblematical traditions of poetry is important: See George Monteiro and Barton L. St. Armand, "The Experienced Emblem: A Study of the Poetry of Emily Dickinson," *Prospects* 6 (1981): 187–280. Perhaps even more crucial are Susan Howe's studies of Dickinson's manipulation of the spatial relations of her manuscript books and pages. See Marjorie Perloff's *The Futurist Moment. Avant Garde, Avant Guerre, and the Language of Rupture* (Chicago: University of Chicago Press, 1986) for a comprehensive introduction to the European scene of experimentalist writing. The illustrations in the book may be studied as an index of the "visible" character of the work of European modernism.

9. The only scholar of modernism who seems to have remembered Brown is Cary Nelson; see his excellent study *Repression and Recovery. Modern American Poetry and the Politics of Cultural Memory 1910–1945* (Madison: University of Wisconsin Press, 1989), 171–73. Nelson's book is also important for its illustrations, which detail some striking physical features in the texts he discusses. But see as well the discussion of Brown in Hugh Ford's *Published in Paris: American and British Writers, Printers, and Publishers in Paris, 1920–1939* (New York: Macmillan, 1975).

10. Cunard bought this font when she purchased William Bird's printing equipment, in order to set up her new press.

11. The famous slogan "the revolution of the word" was applied to the program set forth in Eugene Jolas's important magazine *transition*. Brown's treatise *The Readies* made its first appearance—in an abbreviated version—in the June 1930 issue.

12. Dick Higgins might call Brown's texts "pattern poems"; see his two excellent studies *George Herbert's Pattern Poems: In Their Tradition* (West Glover, Vt., and New York: Unpublished Editions, 1977) and *Pattern Poetry. Guide to an Unknown*

Literature (Albany: State University of New York Press, 1987). But Higgins' pattern poems carry a strong element of Pythagoreanism, and at least an abstract "musicality" which is entirely absent from Brown's texts.

13. *Readies for Bob Brown's Machine* (1931), 162.

14. Ibid., 164.

15. For useful information about the publishing firm see Joe W. Kraus, *Messrs. Copeland and Day* (Philadelphia: George S. MacManus Co., 1979) and Stephen Maxfield Parrish, *Currents of the Nineties in Boston and London* (New York: Garland Publishing Inc., 1987), chap. 3. A curious but startling fact is that Crane was inspired to write his innovative free verse poems after hearing William Dean Howells give a reading from Emily Dickinson's recently published poetry. See Parrish, 268.

16. A few of the poems run beyond a single page. In no case, however, does a page print any part of another poem.

17. *The Paris Tribune* for 13 January 1930 noted the imminent publication of Brown's book and gave a brief account of his idea for a reading machine. See *The Left Bank Revisited: Selections from The Paris Tribune 1917–1934*, edited with an introduction by Hugh Ford (University Park and London: Pennsylvania State University Press, 1972), 122.

18. *Pythagorean Silence* is a meditation on war and violence. Pearl Harbor figures centrally in the work because of Howe's (and her father's) personal involvement with that event—historical and biographical facts which are woven into the drama of the work.

19. *Pythagorean Silence* has been printed twice, first in 1982 as a Montemora Supplement. There it is printed by itself in an unpaginated text. Sun & Moon Press reissued the poem in 1990 in *The Europe of Trusts*, a collection of three works with an introduction by Howe. There the text is paginated. In both cases, however, the page I am discussing here comes as a verso.

20. In "There Are Not Leaves Enough To Crown To Cover To Crown To Cover," her introduction to *The Europe of Trusts*.

21. Howe is also probably playing on the word "wood" and intending us to hear the verbal form of the optative mood.

22. The quotations in this imbedded dialogue are from an anonymous set of criticisms made to an earlier version of the text.

23. See "Method and L=A=N=G=U=A=G=E," in *In the American Tree*, ed. Ron Silliman (Orono, Maine: National Poetry Foundation, 1986), 612.

24. *Artifice of Absorption* is Bernstein's *ars poetica* printed as a special issue of *Paper Air* (4:1, 1987); for a discussion of Bernstein's work see Anne Mack, J. J. Rome, Georg Mannejc, "Private Enigmas and Critical Functions, with Particular Reference to the Work of Charles Bernstein," *New Literary History* 22 (Spring 1991): 443–64.

25. "Disappearance of the Word, Appearance of the World," in *The New Sentence* (New York: Roof Books, 1987), 8.

26. Ibid.

27. See *The Collected Books of Jack Spicer*, ed. and with a commentary by Robin Blaser (Santa Rosa: Black Sparrow Press, 1989), 382.

28. Ibid.

29. Charles Bernstein, "Living Tissue/Dead Ideas," in *Content's Dream. Essays 1975–1984* (Los Angeles: Sun & Moon Press, 1986), 368. Hereafter cited in the text as *CD*.

30. Seth Lerer has pointed out the possibility of taking the title as an imperative rather than a noun phrase.

31. XXX's reading of "Lift Off" was written by an anonymous press reader of *Black Riders*. I have transcribed the core of the reader's (excellent) commentary.

32. Like Morris and Pound, both have been actively involved in every aspect of poetry's production—from writing to book design to editing to distribution.

33. *After Lorca*. With an introduction by Federico Garcia Lorca (San Francisco: White Rabbit Press, 1957), 56. See also Spicer's exemplary remark: "Prose invents— poetry discloses" (4).

34. Spicer, *Language* (San Francisco: White Rabbit Press, 1965), 27.

35. "Thing Language" is not properly speaking the "title" of this text, but the section heading for the poetic sequence of which the quoted text is the first part. See Spicer's *Language*, [iii], 1.

36. Most notable are the following: First, the text is printed high on the page and leaves a considerable white space below—about twice as much white space as the space occupied by the printed text (one recalls Stephen Crane's arrangement of his *Black Riders* poems); second, the page bears the number 1 as a centered footer, a sign emphasizing the sequential integrity of the section titled "Thing Language." The section is the first part of the book *Language*.

CHAPTER 3

1. This crisis has been widely debated; my own contribution to the discussion may be found in *Social Values and Poetic Acts* (Cambridge, Mass.: Harvard University Press, 1987). The critique of Plato in the early sections of this work is particularly relevant to the question of poetry's truth functions. The same subject is pursued further in the sequel to *Social Values*, *Towards a Literature of Knowledge* (Oxford University Press and University of Chicago Press, 1989).

2. *Poetry and Truth. The Beloit Lectures and Poems*, transcribed and edited by George Butterick (San Francisco: Four Seasons Foundation, 1971). These texts are often extremely suggestive and interesting, but their loose, rambling manner betrays Olson's lack of intellectual clarity.

3. Michael Davidson, "Palimtexts: Postmodern Poetry and the Material Text," *Genre* 20 (Fall–Winter 1987): 307–28; Rachel Blau Du Plessis, ed., "The Anthropologist of Myself: a selection from working papers [of George Oppen]," *Sulfur* 26 (Spring 1990): 135–164.

4. "Laura Riding," *Kenyon Review* no. 3 (Summer, 1939): 342.

5. "To the Reader," in *Collected Poems* (New York: Random House, 1938), xviii. Hereafter cited in the text as *Collected Poems*.

6. Barbara Adams has pointed to a "single exception," "a poem she 'forgot' she wrote in the form of a letter to a friend in 1978" (*The Enemy Self. Poetry and Criticism of Laura Riding* [Ann Arbor and London: UMI Research Press, 1990], 110. This

work, *How a Poem Comes to Be*, "was published in 1980 as a broadside in a signed, limited edition" (ibid.).

7. Riding has expressed her critique of poetry in various terms. In *The Telling* (New York: Harper and Row, 1973), for instance, she says that "poetry seems to me to have been reduced to verbal theatrics and separated from its identity as literature's fountain-head of spiritual seriousness" (168). Or, more absolutely: "Poetry . . . never breaks forth from the tellers: the telling travels round and round the tellers in stand-still coils, a bemusement in which tellers and listeners are lost" (11). See also pp. 65–67.

8. The last, and deliberately culminant, section of the *Collected Poems* is headed "Poems Continual."

9. See, for example, Joyce Piell Wexler's *Laura Riding's Pursuit of Truth* (Athens: Ohio University Press, 1979), chapter 11, especially pp. 146–51.

10. See: "diction (or 'style') must be concerned, fundamentally, with our need of speaking to one another the ultimate confidences, in the exchange of which, only, do we know, and can we be, all we as human are" (ibid.).

11. This text is from "Excerpts from a Recording (1972), Explaining the Poems," printed in *The Poems of Laura Riding. A New Edition of the 1938 Collection* (New York: Persea Books, 1980), 417 (hereafter cited as *Persea*).

12. See Bernstein's "The Telling," in *Content's Dream. Essays 1975–1984* (Los Angeles: Sun & Moon Press, 1986), 340–42 (reprinted from *Poetry Project Newsletter*, January 1977), where he specifically addresses himself to Riding's challenge.

13. "The Chinese Notebook" (no. 190), in *The Age of Huts* (New York: Roof Books, 1986), 63.

14. Silliman has set forth a general theory for these kinds of texts in his volume *The New Sentence* (New York: Roof Books, 1987). See especially sections 2 and 3 where Silliman sketches a history for this kind of "prose poetry." A few notable examples of these borderline texts are Carla Harryman's *Property*, Tuumba chapbooks no. 39 (Berkeley: Tuumba, 1982), David Bromige's *My Poetry* (Berkeley: The Figures, 1980), Lyn Hejinian's *My Life*, 2d ed. (Los Angeles: Sun & Moon Press, 1987), many of Alan Davies' works, and Susan Howe's *My Emily Dickinson* (Berkeley: North Atlantic Books, 1985).

15. Davies' "Language Mind Writing" is printed complete in his collection *Signage* (New York: Roof Books, 1987), 121–33. Howe's book is printed by North Atlantic Books (Berkeley, 1985).

16. See Silliman, *The New Sentence*. See n. 14.

17. See Stephen Fredman, *Poet's Prose: The Crisis in American Poetry* (Cambridge and New York: Cambridge University Press, 1983).

18. In his essay "The New Sentence" Silliman lists eight specific characteristics of "new sentence writing" (see *The New Sentence*, 91). In this paragraph I am generalizing what I take to be their common elements.

19. (New York: Grove Press, 1988), 113.

20. The poet/theoretician whose thought most closely reflects Acker's kind of writing is surely Steve McCaffery. See his *North of Intention. Critical Writings 1973–86* (Toronto: Nightwood Editions, 1986), and especially 143–58, 201–21.

21. See the last three sections of Spicer's *Language* (San Francisco: White Rabbit Press, 1965).

22. See *The Marriage of Heaven and Hell*, pl. 20 (as well as the entire "Memorable Fancy" on pls. 17–20), and his "Annotations to Berkeley's *Siris.*"

23. See *Content's Dream*, 61–86.

24. *Love as Love, Death as Death* (London: Seizin Press, 1928)

25. "The Simply" is the opening poem in Bernstein's recent collection of poetry, *The Sophist* (Los Angeles: Sun & Moon Press, 1987).

26. See Blake's letter to Thomas Butts, 6 July 1803 (in *The Complete Poetry and Prose of William Blake*, ed. David V. Erdman, with commentary by Harold Bloom, newly revised edition (Berkeley and Los Angeles: University of California Press, 1982), 730.

27. Leslie Scalapino, "Note on My Writing," in *How Phenomena Appear to Unfold* (Elmwood, Ct.: Potes and Poets Press, 1989), 21.

CHAPTER 4

1. See Gerald L. Bruns, "The Hermeneutics of Midrash," in *The Book and the Text: The Bible and Literary Theory*, ed. Regina Schwartz (Oxford: Basil Blackwell, 1990), 196–97.

2. See Keats's letter to Benjamin Bailey, 22 Nov. 1817, in *The Letters of John Keats*, ed. Hyder Edward Rollins (Cambridge, Mass.: Harvard University Press, 1958), 1:43.

3. See "A Defence of Poetry," in *Shelley's Prose, or The Trumpet of a Prophecy*, ed. David Lee Clark (Albuquerque: University of New Mexico Press, 1954), 294.

4. See S. T. Coleridge, *Biographia Literaria*, ed. James Engell and W. Jackson Bate (Princeton: Princeton University Press, 1983), 1:304.

5. See *The Marriage of Heaven and Hell*, plate 11.

6. Mannejc here quotes variously from Herbert F. Tucker's important essay "Dramatic Monologue and the Overhearing of Lyric," in *Lyric Poetry. Beyond New Criticism*, ed. Chaviva Hosek and Patricia Parker (Ithaca and London: Cornell University Press, 1985), 228.

7. Ibid., 234.

8. Mannejc quotes from Ashton Nichols, "Dialogism in the Dramatic Monologue: Suppressed Voices in Browning," *Victorians Institute Journal* 18 (1990): 36. Nichols's essay acknowledges a profound debt to Tucker's earlier work.

9. Ibid., 47.

10. Ibid., 45.

11. Ibid., 45–46.

12. In the first edition of *Dramatic Lyrics* (1842) the poem was titled simply "*I. Italy*"—the roman numeral signaling that the poem was being paired with the following work, which was titled "*II. France.*" The pairing was further emphasized in the table of contents, where the two were indicated under the heading "Italy and France." For a good discussion see William Clyde DeVane, *A Browning Handbook*, 2d ed. (New York: Appleton-Century-Crofts Inc., 1955), 107.

13. See Plato's *Protagoras*, 347c–348a.

14. See *Brecht on Theatre. The Development of an Aesthetic*, ed. and trans. John Willett (New York: Hill and Wang, 1964), 71.

15. Ibid., 44. The emphasis here is McGrem's, not Brecht's.

16. Ibid., 71.

17. Ibid., 71.

Afterword

1. "Literal Language," in *New Literary History* 22 (Summer 1991): 603–11.

2. Bezeczky's quotes from Ricoeur's *The Rule of Metaphor*, trans. Robert Czerny (Toronto, 1977), 22.

3. A revisionist movement has been underway for ten years or so. Three of its most notable scholarly voices are Houston Baker, Cary Nelson, and Marjorie Perloff.

Index